Worst Constitutional Liars

DOUGLAS V. GIBBS

Constitution Association Press: Murrieta, California

ISBN:1985398133
ISBN-13:9781985398139

To America

ABOUT THE AUTHOR

Douglas V. Gibbs is a Radio Host, Author, Instructor, Television Contributor, Columnist, Public Speaker, Blogger, Editor, Fellow of the American Freedom Alliance, Director of Civics and Constitution Studies for the National Congress of Racial Equality, President of the Constitution Association, Secretary of Birth Choice Centers Inc. (Temecula and Hemet locations), board member of the Murrieta-Temecula Republican Assembly & California Republican Assembly, a member of the American Authors Association & Military Writers Society of America, a United States Navy Veteran, husband, father, grandfather, and advocate for honest government.

OTHER BOOKS BY DOUGLAS V. GIBBS

- *25 Myths of the United States Constitution*

- *The Basic Constitution: An Examination of the Principles and Philosophies of the United States Constitution.*

- *Silenced Screams: Abortion in a Virtuous Society*

- *Concepts of the U.S. Constitution*

- *5 Solutions to Save America*

COMING SOON

- *A Promise of American Liberty*

- *Tyrant's Guide to Killing Liberty*

CONTENTS

DOUGLAS V. GIBBS

• The List that Could Have Been

The list of influential Americans (and a few non-Americans), both living and dead, who have had a negative impact on our constitutional republic, and who have been a dire threat to the constitutional philosophies and principles upon which this country was founded, is extensive. If I were to write a book filled with extensive histories about each and every one of them, the final product would be massive, and would dwarf even the most outrageously voluminous pieces of legislation ever to work its way through the halls of the United States Congress. However, while I limited the list of Constitutional Liars to seven for the purpose of the title of this book, and really ten if you count the honorable mentions and post script, I did want to make a quick reference to other figures who have posed as threats to our U.S. Constitution throughout history, and explain why they did not make the final list as constitutional liars.

Understand, the list of seven (plus three) was comprised based upon the premise that the individuals listed were "constitutional liars," not merely purveyors of unconstitutional concepts and actions. Saul Alinsky, for example, could be listed as among the greatest threats to our constitutional way of life, but he never claimed to be a supporter or champion of the Constitution, therefore, he was never really a constitutional liar. I suppose you could say that instead of being constitutional liars, some of the people on this first list could be classified as devout enemies of the United States Constitution (or at least enemies of the *laissez faire* principles upon which the document was fashioned).

○ **Jean-Jacques Rousseau**, 1712-1778: Rousseau's violent and revolutionary ideology of collectivism called for a homogeneous society compliant with utopian communitarianism. His support for concepts such as "The General Will," which demanded obedience to the ruling elite so that man may be "forced to be free,"[1] served as fuel for the revolutionary tide being carried out by the French Jacobins during the approach, and fulfillment, of the French Revolution. Much of Europe's current political thought finds its foundation in Rousseau's writings of adherence to a statist philosophy that Karl Marx would later mold into a manifesto of modern communism. Rousseau was influential on one of America's Founding Fathers, Alexander Hamilton, who was trusted by George Washington, and who used that trust to negatively influence the economic system of the United States during the early years of the country after the ratification of the United States Constitution, and to instill a system of implied law, which ultimately led to judicial review, and the belief that the U.S. Constitution is a living and breathing document that changes with the whims of society, and the opinions of judges and politicians.

○ **Meyer Amschel Rothschild**, 1744-1812: Son of Amschel Moses Bauer (who would later change his name to "Rothschild"); was one part of a very powerful European banking family. Meyer Rothschild was sent to Frankfurt, Germany by his father to operate a banking house, as his four brothers were sent to other locations in Europe to do the same. The action ensured that the Rothschild Family was privy to immediate information about major events in Europe, often even before rulers of the countries involved, giving the Rothschilds an early advantage in the marketplace. The power accumulated until eventually the Rothschild Family became powerful players in Europe (and eventually worldwide), making them king-makers and nation killers through economic manipulation and financial threats. Meyer Rothschild became known, as the power of the Rothschild Family grew, for the quote, "Permit me to control the money of a nation, and I care not who makes its laws." The Rothschild family became instrumental in the forming of the Second Bank of the United States in yet another attempt to drag the U.S. financial system into Europe, and into their control. During the charter of the Second Bank of the United States, Meyer Rothschild used constant influence to help shape U.S. policy, and usher the republic towards a pure democracy, during the early 19th Century, and beyond.[2]

○ **John Jay**, 1745-1829: The first Chief Justice of the United States who turned down a later opportunity to hold that office in 1801 when it was offered by President John Adams. Jay had originally vacated his position as Chief Justice of the United States when he was elected Governor of New York. After Jay's term as governor ended, during the waning months of Adams' presidency where the Federalist Party had lost the White House and both Houses of Congress to Thomas Jefferson and his Republicans after the 1800 Election, Adams offered Jay the opportunity to return as Chief Justice. Jay turned down the opportunity, indicating that he considered the nature of the position to be powerless and that it lacked the "energy, weight, and dignity which are essential to its affording due support to the national government."[3] Jay disagreed with the notion by the delegates of the Constitutional Convention that the judicial branch should be the weakest of the three branches of government.[4] As a proponent of strong, centralized government, Jay worked as a supporter of the Constitution in the hopes it would be ratified by New York in 1788 by pseudonymously writing five of the several Federalist papers,[5] believing that the creation of the federal government was at least a step in the right direction, even though he was disappointed that so many limitations existed in the document regarding the federal government's authorities on internal issues.

○ **John D. Rockefeller**, 1839-1937: An early refiner of oil, John D. Rockefeller's rise began in 1863 with two partners. Rockefeller sought to become the largest refiner in the world, and perhaps the only refiner in the world, and by 1879 he controlled ninety-five percent of the oil being refined in the United States. His ambition then shifted to that of an international oil monopoly. While working to develop a large oil reserve in Russia, Rockefeller teamed up with the Rothschild Family, bringing Russia into the industrialized world. Thanks to Rockefeller, during the period between 1907 and 1913, Russia's growth in industrial production exceeded that of the United States. When the 1917 Russian Revolution brought communism to the region, Rockefeller agreed to support the plan to eliminate the Czar, playing a large part in instigating the violence that accompanied the revolution.[6] John D. Rockefeller's son, John D. Rockefeller, Jr., was a participant and instrumental voice in the creation of the U.S. Federal Reserve (which began with a secret meeting on Jekyll Island in 1910[7], and led to the Federal Reserve Act in 1913). Nelson Aldrich Rockefeller, son of John D. Rockefeller, Jr., became Vice President of the United States in 1974, but his bid to replace Richard Nixon after Nixon's second-term ended was upended when a contrived ploy of Watergate, which had been intended to deliver the White House to the unelectable Nelson Rockefeller, was discovered and exposed.[8]

○ **Eugene Debs**, 1855–1926: An early leader of the labor movement, organizing one of the United States' first industrial unions, the American Railway

Union (1893). Debs was a five-time candidate for President of the United States as a member of the Socialist Party. He popularized ideas about government's alleged role in guaranteeing various rights and liberties, in complete defiance of the limited authorities granted to the federal government by the U.S. Constitution. He led the Pullman Strike of 1894. On September 14, 1918, Debs was sentenced to ten years in a Federal penitentiary for treason under the Espionage Law of June 15, 1917. On March 10, 1919, after a series of appeals, Debs was advised that the Supreme Court had upheld the decision of the lower court, after which he surrendered to Federal police in Cleveland, Ohio. On April 19, 1919, five months after the World War had ended, Debs entered Moundsville jail in West Virginia, since the Federal jails were too crowded with political prisoners to accommodate him. He was later transferred to the penitentiary at Atlanta. In 1920, Debs was nominated to run as a candidate for the presidency of the United States from behind prison bars as a socialist. Two years and nine months after he had entered prison, Debs was pardoned, and on December 25, 1921 he stepped out of the jail and into freedom, all along refusing to recant his revolutionary principles.[9]

∘ **John Dewey** (1859–1952). A philosopher, psychologist and education reformer, Dewey was an engaged activist, a prolific writer for popular magazines and the leading exemplar of American pragmatism. He founded the "laboratory school" at the University of Chicago to put his ideas about progressive education into practice. His ideas about "experiential learning" influenced several generations of educators. An early supporter of teachers' unions and academic freedom, he spoke out and organized against efforts to restrict freedom of ideas, helped found the NAACP and supported women's suffrage. Today's progressive grip on the education system is larger due to the infiltration by leftism initiated by John Dewey.[10]

○ **Upton Sinclair,** 1878–1968: An award winning author, Sinclair wrote ninety books, most of which were novels claiming to expose social injustice, or they were launched direct attacks against allegedly powerful institutions like religion, the new industry, and oil companies. In 1934 he departed from the Socialist Party, consequently winning the Democratic nomination for governor of California on a platform to "end poverty in California." Sinclair lost, but his campaign mobilized millions of voters, which is believed to have helped push Franklin Delano Roosevelt to the left, leading Roosevelt to become an enemy of the Constitution in the hopes that circumventing the document may enable him to usher into the United States a non-violent socialist revolution.[11]

○ **Margaret Sanger,** 1879–1966: A eugenicist, and the founder of Planned Parenthood in 1921.[12] In 1912 she first launched her crusade as an advocate for birth control, which included her racist desire to limit the birthrate of those who she considered to be "human weeds".[13] She wrote articles on health for the Socialist Party paper *The Call* and wrote several books. In 1916 she set up the first birth control clinic in the United States. Her influence led generations of socialists to call for the legalization of abortion,[14] and to do so nationally despite the lack of constitutional authority to the federal government. 2016 Presidential Candidate Hillary Clinton, in March of 2009 while she was Secretary of State of the United States, accepted a Planned Parenthood Margaret Sanger Award. During her speech, Mrs. Clinton stated, "I admire Margaret Sanger enormously, her courage, her tenacity, her vision…I am really in awe of her."[15]

○ **Roger Baldwin,** 1884–1981: A pacifist and socialist who founded the American Civil Liberties Union in 1917. The organization was originally called the National Civil Liberties Bureau. The organization was originally created to defend the rights of antiwar conscientious objectors. Baldwin served as its executive director until 1950.[16] The ACLU has become a constant enemy of the original intent of the United States Constitution, doing so in the name of constitutional rights, while supporting progressive government intrusion through court cases and political influence. In 2014 the ACLU called for President Barack Obama to unconstitutionally grab executive power in an effort to force local and state law enforcement to comply with racially biased guidelines.[17]

○ **Frances Perkins,** 1880–1965: Labor secretary under Franklin Roosevelt, advocating for Social Security, the minimum wage, workers' right to unionize, and other New Deal reforms. She marched in suffrage parades and gave street-corner speeches in favor of women's suffrage. She originally joined the Socialist Party, but later switched to the Democrat Party.[18]

○ **Norman Thomas**, 1884–1968: A very visible socialist during the 1930s through the 1950s. He called his crusade, since he was an ordained Presbyterian minister, the "social gospel". During World War I he joined the Socialist Party. He served as associate editor for *The Nation*, co-director of the League for Industrial Democracy, and was a founder of the National Civil Liberties Bureau (which later changed its name to the American Civil Liberties Union - ACLU). He ran for governor, mayor, State Senate and City Council on the Socialist Party ticket. He ran for president six times. His revolutionary socialist ideas were in constant conflict with the philosophies and authorities granted by the United States Constitution.[19]

○ **Henry Wallace**, 1888–1965: Wallace was President Franklin Delano Roosevelt's agriculture secretary (1933–40) and then vice president (1940–44). He played an important role in promoting Roosevelt's New Deal initiatives, which on their face violated the authorities granted by the United States Constitution. He also served as editor of *The*

New Republic. Wallace ran for president in 1948 on the Progressive Party ticket. Some Democrats believed Wallace's socialist positions to be too radical, and worried that his campaign as a progressive would split the vote enough to jeopardize Truman's campaign. By the end of the election, Wallace received less than 2 percent of the popular vote.[20]

○ **Nelson Aldrich Rockefeller**, 1908 – 1979: Nelson Aldrich Rockefeller, son of John D. Rockefeller, Jr., became Vice President of the United States in 1974, but his bid to replace Richard Nixon after Nixon's second-term ended was upended when a contrived ploy of Watergate, which had been intended to deliver the White House to the unelectable Nelson Rockefeller, was discovered and exposed. In 1962, during a lecture at Harvard University, Nelson Rockefeller said, "...a new and free order [is] struggling to be born...(There is a) fever of nationalism...(but) the nation-state is becoming less and less competent to perform its international political tasks...These are some of the reasons pressing us to lead vigorously toward the true building of a new world order...(with) voluntary service...Sooner perhaps than we may realize...there will evolve the bases for a federal structure of the free world."[21]   Rockefeller's globalist worldview conflicted with the concept of American exceptionalism, and the concept held by the Framers of the U.S. Constitution regarding foreign entanglements.

◦ **Saul Alinsky**, 1909–1972: A community organizer, Marxist activist, and author of *Reveille for Radicals* (1946) and *Rules for Radicals* (1971). His tactics, largely presented in detail in his books, have influenced leftist activists over that last few decades. Many believe recent politicians like Hillary Clinton and Barack Obama to be students of Alinsky's radical methods – methods that may be at the foundation of recent violent protests by groups like Black Lives Matter, and Antifa. Alinsky believed the Constitution to be an obstacle to revolution.[22]

◦ **Earl Warren,** 1891–1974: Warren served as chief justice on the United States Supreme Court from 1953 to 1969. He led a group of leftist justices in their effort to expand the scope of a variety of cases involving the progressive concept of social justice. Eisenhower nominated Warren to the Supreme Court, believing that since Warren claimed to be a Republican, he was a conservative jurist. Eisenhower later famously proclaimed that appointing Warren was the "biggest damn fool mistake" he'd ever made.[23] In *Reynolds v. Sims* (1964) Chief Justice Warren led the Supreme Court to pressure States to abide by the national model established by the 17th Amendment. The 17th Amendment, which had been ratified in 1913, changed the appointment of U.S. Senators by the State legislatures to a democratic vote by the people. At the State level, State Assembly members were voted in by the public, but the State Senators appointment had followed the federal model by giving the appointment of State Senators as a responsibility of the County leadership. Senate Districts, as a result, were consistent with county boundaries, regardless of population. In *Reynolds v. Sims*, the Warren Court ordered the States to abandon their practice of republicanism, and instead embrace democracy by redrawing Senate District lines to provide a fair apportionment of the legislature, and then for the State Senators to be voted into office by the voters of the new districts.[24] The ruling not only violated the concept of Separation of Powers when Warren's Supreme Court legislated from the bench, but it also violated Article IV., Section 4 of the United States Constitution, which states that the "United States shall guarantee to every State in his Union a Republican Form of Government."

○ **Harry Hay**, 1912–2002: Hay co-founded the first major gay rights organization in the United States in 1950. During the 1930s and 1940s, Hay was a member of the Communist Party. He organized the first semipublic homosexual discussion group in 1950, which soon became the Mattachine Society. In 1953 he helped start *ONE*, a magazine addressing homosexuality's political influence, and drive for acceptance in mainstream culture. Since then, the gay agenda has sought a variety of misapplications of the U.S. Constitution in order to judicially coerce society to abide by the demands of homosexual activists.[25]

7 WORST CONSTITUTIONAL LIARS

○ **Howard Zinn**, 1922-2010: Author of "A People's History of the United States," a book that alleges to provide a history of the United States from the point of view of those oppressed by the U.S. Constitution and the American System, as a tale of imperialism (compounding the concept that the Mexican-American War was a war of expansionism, rather than liberation from the iron fist of Mexican Dictator Antonio Lopez de Santa Anna), or a tale of unjust treatment of socialists like Eugene Debs who was, according to Zinn, jailed for truthfully exclaiming World War I, for the Americans, was a war of conquest and plunder. Born the son of immigrants from Russia and Ukraine, Zinn's fondness for history (he earned a Ph.D. in history from Columbia University) and Marxism led him to become an activist with a "flair for the theatrical" and with "genius at engaging an audience," which "won him numerous speaking invitations and requests from leftist causes...Zinn's radical view of history looked cynically at American motives abroad and benignly on the Soviet Union's. He relentlessly criticized American policy...and declared that historical research should be carried out to serve present-day political ends...Zinn expressed his radicalism through activism..."[26] In *A People's History of the United States*, he presented the U.S. Constitution through the eyes of the slaves, suggesting the founding document to be racist and oppressive at its very foundation.

○ **Henry Kissinger**, b. 1923: A Jewish refugee who fled Nazi Germany in 1938, he arrived in New York on September 5, 1938 as a teenager. He excelled academically, but his educational pursuits were interrupted when he was drafted into the U.S. Army in 1943. While stationed in South Carolina, Kissinger naturalized as a U.S. Citizen, and then was assigned to the military intelligence section of his division. He volunteered for hazardous intelligence duties, which placed him in the fight during the Battle of the Bulge. In Hanover he was in charge of a team tasked with tracking down Gestapo officers, and other saboteurs, for which he was assigned the Bronze Star. After the war he continued his education, ultimately earning his Masters Degree and Ph.D. at Harvard University.[27] He became a member of the faculty at Harvard, later branching out as a consultant to the National Security Council's Operations Coordinating Board (A committee under the Executive Branch of the United States Government responsible for integrating the implementation of national security policies across several agencies), and study director in nuclear weapons and foreign policy at the Council on Foreign Relations. He served as National Security Advisor and Secretary of State under President Richard Nixon, and continued as Secretary of State under President Gerald Ford. After the election of President Jimmy Carter, Kissinger left public office, but continued to participate in the Council on Foreign Relations and the Trilateral Commission, while also maintaining his role in political counseling.[28]

George H.W. Bush, b. 1924: The 41st President of the United States from 1989 to 1993. He was the Vice President under President Ronald Reagan from 1981 to 1989. Prior to his time in the executive branch, Bush served as a congressman, director of the CIA, and as a U.S. Navy Aviator during World War II.[29] As President of the United States, amidst growing opposition to corporate internationalism, President George H.W. Bush, in a speech, "Toward a New World Order", delivered on September 11, 1990 during a joint session of Congress, described his objectives for post-Cold War global governance in cooperation with post-Soviet states. He said, "Until now, the world we've known has been a world divided—a world of barbed wire and concrete block, conflict and cold war. Now, we can see a new world coming into view. A world in which there is the very real prospect of a new world order..."[30] The Founding Fathers warned against compromising the sovereignty of the United States and engaging in foreign entanglements.[31] The American System was established on the principles of individual liberty, not collective communalism. That said, the Framers of the Constitution also used the term "New World Order," but meant it in a different manner.[32] Their definition was one regarding liberty, and the spread of American ideals not through imperialism, but by example and imitation.

○ **James Earl Carter, Jr.** (Jimmy Carter), b. 1924: After two terms in the Georgia State Senate, and as the 76th Governor of the State of Georgia, James "Jimmy" Carter served as the 39th President of the United States from 1977 to 1981.[33] In 2002, Carter was a Nobel Peace Prize recipient.[34] Carter served in the United States Navy from 1943 to 1953, and as a reservist from 1953 to 1961. He is the only United States Naval Academy graduate to be elected to the White House.[35] As President, Carter pardoned all evaders of the Vietnam War drafts.[36] Also during his administration, the Departments of Energy and Education were unconstitutionally established.[37] Near the end of his tenure as President, American citizens were held hostage in Iran (1979-1981).[38] After his presidency ended, in 1982, he founded the Carter Center, which played an active role in human rights and disease prevention on a global scale.[39] Internationalism has never been anything new to Carter. Zbigniew Brzezinski, who would serve as Carter's National Security Advisor, and David Rockefeller, recruited Carter for membership in the Trilateral Commission in 1976, and then with the Trilateralist's assistance, Carter rocketed out of nowhere into victory in the Democrat National Primaries, and ultimately to the White House the same year. Carter stacked his administration with Trilateralists, and then used his presidency to assist communist regimes throughout the world.[40] Among the most notable international moves was when Carter pressured the government of once prosperous Rhodesia to step aside so that communist Robert

Mugabe could be put into power.[41] Since the country's sharp left turn, it has changed its name to Zimbabwe, and has become a land of hyperinflation, oppression, crime waves, hunger, poverty, and a source of a mass exodus of refugees seeking to escape. Carter's proxy army in Afghanistan deliberately provoked the 1979 Soviet invasion of the country,[42] and then his administration followed up with the boycott of the 1980 Moscow Olympics.[43] Carter's abandonment of the nationalist American-friendly Nicaraguan government ultimately brought the Cuba-backed communist Sandinistas into power.[44] The anti-constitution and pro-globalism antics of Carter have continued through the new millennium, including support for Barack Obama's Organizing for America, and his criticism against any opposition to Islam or socialism, with no signs of slowing down until he eventually, finally, meets his Maker – whenever that may be.

○ **Zbigniew Brzezinski,** 1928–2017: Polish-American diplomat and scientist who served as counselor to President Lyndon B. Johnson (1966-1968) and National Security Advisor to President Jimmy Carter (1977-1981). He was involved in normalizing ties with the People's Republic of China, and severing ties with Free China (Republic of China on Taiwan). Brzezinski founded the Trilateral Commission in 1973. He is also a member of the Council on Foreign Relations. While Brzezinski has espoused hatred for Russia, he is not necessarily against socialism. He has been one of the forces behind the United Nations' globalist version of Marxism. Brzezinski openly praises Marxism in his book *Between Two Ages*, published in 1970 – a system that will control man's behavior and mind, according to his book, through "brain chipping" in a "technetronic" dictatorship. Brzezinski has also been an architect in encouraging joint American and Muslim networks, as well as providing funding and training for the Taliban and al Qaeda terrorist groups.[45]

○ **Noam Chomsky**, b. 1928: The author of over 100 books covering linguistics, war, politics, mass media, and his alignment with socialism, Chomsky was an outspoken opponent of the Vietnam War, which he viewed as being an act of American imperialism. Chomsky's activism has extended to his opposition to the War on Terror, and his support for the *Occupy Movement*. His work has been influential in the anti-capitalism and anti-imperialist movements, and he has been an ardent supporter of socialist politician Bernie Sanders. In 2011, using an argument in favor of democracy as a means to achieve socialism, Chomsky said, "The guiding principle (for American government) is that as long as the public is under control, everything is fine. (The traditional argument is) the powerful should gain ends by any possible means. As long as the public is kept under control, public will doesn't matter." His argument sounds like simply another version of Marx's "Workers of the world, unite!"[46]

◦ **Harvey Milk**, 1930–1978: In 1977 Milk was elected to San Francisco's Board of Supervisors, which provided him with two distinctions; the first openly gay elected official in California and the most visible gay politician in the country. Milk was a charismatic homosexual activist who was later assassinated by a political rival. [47] Emboldened by Milk's activism, the homosexual agenda has reached a point of being willing to violate the rights of others (i.e. religious rights, right to free speech) through coercive unconstitutional methods in order to normalize homosexuality and advance their agenda.

◦ **Ralph Nader**, b. 1934: Known for his work in environmentalism, Nader ran for president four times. His run in 2000 was considered controversial by Democrats because, as a Green Party candidate, he won a significant number of votes in Florida that many believe may have cost Democrat Al Gore the election.[48] While Nader demands that the federal government does something about the environment, until an amendment is ratified giving the federal government the authority, there's nothing the federal government can legally do.

◦ **Gloria Steinem,** b. 1934: A radical feminist and supporter of abortion, in 1970 she led the Women's Strike for Equality march in New York, and in 1972 she founded *Ms.* magazine, which became a leading feminist publication at the time. She remains a polarizing figure in media, continuing her presence as a writer, and with appearances on television. She co-founded the National Women's Political Caucus, the Ms. Foundation for Women, Choice USA, the Women's Media Center and the Coalition of Labor Union Women.[49]

○ **Alan Dershowitz**, b. 1938: During an appearance on Newsmax TV in 2015, Harvard Law Professor Emeritus Alan Dershowitz said the 2nd Amendment is an "absurd thing" in our constitution and that our legal framework needs to be adjusted "to create a presumption against gun ownership instead of a presumption in favor of gun ownership."[50]   An ideological liberal leftist, Dershowitz is an author of a number of books regarding politics and law, including *Rights from Wrongs: A Secular Theory of the Origins of Rights*.[51] While an avowed supporter of the Democrat party, he has criticized the Democrats for their case against Trump's alleged ties to Russia, and has stated there is "no case" for obstruction of justice against President Trump regarding the firing of former FBI Director James Comey.[52]   In 2016, he said he would leave the Democrat Party if Keith Ellison was appointed party chair.[53]   Communist Tom Perez was appointed, instead, a choice Dershowitz was fine with. He claims he's a "defender of individual rights" and a Constitutional Scholar. However, his definitions of constitutional law betray the Framers, and are not based on the original intent of the document.

○ **Tom Hayden**, b. 1939: Founder of Students for a Democratic Society (a socialist organization) in

1960, Hayden worked as a community organizer in Newark with student activists and other leftists as an antiwar demonstrator. His trips to Cambodia and North Vietnam with the intent to directly challenge American military involvement in Southeast Asia was viewed by some to be treasonous at best. A 1960s radical activist, he challenged Senator John Tunney of California in the Democratic primary of 1976. Later elected to the California legislature, he served for eighteen years as an environmental and consumer advocate.[54]

○ **Bernie Sanders**, b. 1941: A U.S. Senator for the State of Vermont since 2007. He caucuses with the Democrat Party, and ran as a Democrat in the 2016 Presidential Election.[55] He considers himself a democratic socialist and a New Deal-era American progressive.[56] A graduate of the University of Chicago in 1964, he was active in the Civil Rights Movement, and served as a member of the U.S. House of Representatives from 1991 until 2007, after he was elected to the Senate in 2006.[57] Sanders' book, Our Revolution: A Future to Believe In, released in November of 2016, lays out his socialist plans for the United States, and it debuted on The New York Times Best Seller list at number 3.[58] Noam Chomsky has described Sanders as being "a New Dealer."[59]

○ **Jesse Jackson**, b. 1941: A polarizing figure in the civil rights arena, Jackson has been a candidate for the Democratic presidential nomination in 1984 and

1988. Jackson's use of boycotts and other pressure tactics are well known, as is his repeated use of the race card. Jackson wrote in September of 2017 that "Voter suppression has a long and shameful history in America. Initially, only white male property owners could vote."[60] The assertion, in an attempt to convince his readers that Voter ID laws, which are designed to protect the vote against fraud, is based on a false assumption. While it is true that in the early elections the States only allowed property owners to vote, this did not limit voting to only white males. In the north, some free black property owners voted, though societal pressure often kept that number low.[61] In the frontier not only were blacks afforded the vote, but nearly every western State or territory also enfranchised women long before women won the privilege to vote in the eastern States.[62] While in the 15th, 19th, 24th and 26th, Amendments, voting is called a "right," the Framers of the Constitution did not consider voting a right. It was seen as a privilege of citizenship, as supported by Article IV. where the Constitution refers to "privileges and immunities," of which voting is among the "privileges" of citizenship in the several States.

○ **Michael Moore**, b. 1954: An American filmmaker whose works side with socialism, and often praises modern communist regimes.[63] Moore spends as much of his time as he can in front of a camera as he is behind one, frequently spewing his socialist dreams on a variety of television outlets.[64] He also regularly speaks at rallies in the hopes of furthering the socialist viewpoint in regards to economics, and the progressive concept of social justice.

A number of readers, after reading the above list, are likely already thinking, "That's it?" I am sure many of you have a much longer list of enemies of the U.S. Constitution in mind, and I agree that the list is absolutely dizzying in terms of how many people truly belong on that list (Bill and Hillary Clinton come to mind). In fact, according to the book (and film by the same name) by Trevor Loudon, "The Enemies Within," based on their socialist affiliations, 100 members of the House of Representatives and 20 members of the United States Senate would not be able to pass a background check to be a janitor in the same building they meet in as members of the United States Congress. However, in the interest keeping this book to a short, readable length, we will not write paragraphs about each and every one of those hard left Congress Critters who are truly enemies of the United States Constitution. Loudon's book already fills nearly 700 pages regarding The Enemies Within.[66]

DOUGLAS V. GIBBS

• Honorable Mention: Theodore Roosevelt and Woodrow Wilson

Theodore Roosevelt   Woodrow Wilson

The Progressive Era posed a grave threat to the United States Constitution. Defenders of the Progressive Era explain that the time period from about 1890 until the end of the Woodrow Wilson presidency in 1921[1] was designed to overthrow corruption in politics,[2] and that the way to accomplish the deed was to initiate a system of government more in line with direct democracy, along with a strong centralized federal government. Along the way the progressives strengthened the role of the President of the United States (largely through the use of executive orders and self-proclaimed "war powers"), established the Federal Reserve, enacted the 16th and 17th Amendments, established legislation targeting "political machines" and "large corporations", and initiated a litany of programs that allowed government to intrude upon local issues through "social programs" and "social reform."[3]

The emergence of the progressive political movement in the United States over a hundred years ago was largely the result of activism carried out by political leaders who leaned towards the foreign teachings of socialism. The depression of the 1890s helped sway public sentiment towards socialism, when small businesses, farms, and labor movements began asking the government to intercede on their behalf.[4] The list of socialist saviors, who called themselves "progressives" to hide their true nature, includes Presidents Theodore Roosevelt and Woodrow Wilson. The progressive cast of characters is vast, and they all claimed that their aims were based on the very best of intentions. Nonetheless, their opinions were considered to be contrary to prevailing academic opinion of the previous decades,[5] for their political beliefs leaned more towards the teachings of the father of communism, Karl Marx, than the principles of liberty laid out by the Founding Fathers.

The turn of the century was promising industrial change and technological advances that convinced the progressives that the old world order must be swept away. Only a new world order would be able to survive the coming changes. Resolutions for the old problems, and the capacity for managing a rapidly growing congregation of new ones, from the point of view of the progressives, required government intervention to be activated at every level so as to be actively involved in all of the allegedly necessary reforms.[6]   The Constitution, according to the progressives, was outdated, and a dynamic system of direct democracy based on a living and breathing constitution that evolves with the developing wave of social change was the instrument needed to lead the charge into the new century.

The plans of the progressives, however, were at direct odds with the American System as it was established through the original intent of the U.S. Constitution.   The black letter of the law on the pages of the United States Constitution indicates that the federal government's authorities are expressly enumerated, and that the powers of the three branches of government are separate and distinct. The States, as the authors of the Constitution (through their delegates at the convention in Philadelphia, and through their debates during the State ratification conventions) were originally the parents over the federal government.   The central government in Washington, D.C., was established to serve the States and We the People, not the other way around. To guard against potential corruption, a series of checks and balances were established, not only in an effort to limit the power of any one politician or segment of the government apparatus, but also to ensure that the excesses of pure democracy did not engulf the republic.   As with politicians, the people, with too much power, cannot be trusted to keep the system limited and true to its original established functions. The Founding Fathers both feared and despised the destructive nature of pure democracy, and utopianism (progressivism by another name), and specifically wrote the Constitution in the manner it was written so that it may stand the test of time, and resist statist concepts such as the *General Will*, *Jabobinism*, and the impending assault by *progressivism*.[7]

The Progressive Era, appearing scarcely more than 100 years after the ratification of the United States Constitution, sought to challenge the thinking of the Founding Fathers, endeavoring to replace the concept of *laissez faire* with the more modern scheme of collectivism through government schemes that used policies championed by supporters of *Marxism*, and *Fabianism*.

"Efficiency, enterprise, opportunity, individualism, substantial laissez-faire, personal success, material welfare – were all dominant American tradition…in the language of Jefferson…these ideas had been fresh and invigorating; in the language [of the new era] they seemed stale and oppressive."[8]

The attacks against the principles of the United States Constitution were not only foreseen by the Founding Fathers, but by other leaders from other countries.

"Your Republic will be as fearfully plundered and laid waste by barbarians in the twentieth century as the Roman Empire was in the fifth century, with this difference – the Huns and Vandals who ravaged the Roman Empire came from without, and your Huns and Vandals will have been engendered within your own country." – Thomas Macaulay, British Parliamentarian, 1857.[9]

The method employed by the Framers of the Constitution to avoid such a calamity was for the central federal government to be limited in its authorities.

James Madison wrote in Federalist #45[10] that "The powers delegated by the proposed constitution to the federal government are few and defined."

Thomas Jefferson, while not a participant in the Constitutional Convention, was highly influential in the delegation, corresponding often with a number of the participants, including James Madison.[11] During his presidency, Jefferson sought to put into practice the limiting principles of government embedded in America's founding documents.[12]

Legislative accomplishments during the Jefferson Presidency were few and far between, not because it was a failed presidency or because America had a do-nothing Congress, but because the men of that era understood the importance of keeping federal legislation within the scope of the authorities granted by the U.S. Constitution. Jefferson stated that good government was "A noiseless course, not meddling with the affairs of others, unattractive of notice, is a mark that society is going on in happiness. If we can prevent the government from wasting the labors of the people under the pretense of taking care of them, they must become happy."[13] No new laws were needed, according to Jefferson, and the laws that were put into play should not be complicated or fit into some kind of long agenda that politicians believe to be necessary in order to justify their existence.

Thomas Jefferson also stated, "Laws are made for men of ordinary understanding, and should therefore be construed by the ordinary rules of common sense. their meaning is not to be sought for in metaphysical subtleties, which may make any thing mean every thing or nothing; at pleasure."[14]

Jefferson challenged the British Parliament, condemning the legislature across the Atlantic Ocean for writing acts that were "tautologous, involved, and parenthetical jargon." From Jefferson's point of view, British statutes were "barbarous, uncouth, and unintelligible."

James Madison revealed how important it was that the President of the United States served as a check against unconstitutional legislation with his veto of the "Bonus Bill" in 1817,[15] which would have unconstitutionally earmarked federal funding for internal improvements (an obligation that was considered to belong to the individual States). It was never intended for the President to serve as a check against Congress once the law was in place, however. Article II specifies that the President "shall take Care that the Laws be faithfully executed."

President Theodore Roosevelt, over a century later, used executive orders (1,006 of them) to take "independent action." He believed a "strong President" may use executive orders to do anything not specifically prohibited by the Constitution. He injected a forceful energy and enthusiasm into the White House, using his position as a "bully pulpit" (Roosevelt's own words). As one observer noted, "He wanted to be the bride at every wedding; the corpse at every funeral."[16]

In slightly over 100 years, the view of the Constitution had evolved from the doctrine of enumerated powers, which said the federal government could do nothing except what the Constitution authorized, to Roosevelt's progressivism, which said it was the "duty" of the president to do "anything that the needs of the Nation demanded unless such action was forbidden by the Constitution or by Law."[17] Roosevelt later admitted, "I did greatly broaden the use of Executive power."[18]

Woodrow Wilson took office in 1913 after an election during which Theodore Roosevelt (a former Republican) ran as the "Bull Moose Progressive Party" candidate with a specific intent to split the

Republican vote. Incumbent Republican President William Howard Taft rejected the idea of a central bank run by international bankers in charge of America's currency. He refused to support the new Federal Reserve proposal. Democrat Woodrow Wilson vowed to sign the act and was given the presidency through Roosevelt's interference.[19]

In 1913, Wilson signed the Federal Reserve Act, and the States ratified the 16th Amendment (enabling direct taxation against the people) and the 17th Amendment (changing the appointment of U.S. Senators by the State legislatures to a popular vote). The following year, war broke out in Europe. While the United States did not declare war until April of 1917, America was involved in many ways in the War in Europe from the very beginning, primarily through trade.[20]

During the First World War, President Wilson used "war powers" to impose his progressive will against the United States at all levels of American life. Wilson's "implied authority" led him to lead the charge in economic and industrial change, using executive orders and administrative regulations to dismantle Article I, Section 1 of the U.S. Constitution.[21]

Article I, Section 1, declares that "All legislative Powers herein granted shall be vested in a Congress of the United States, which shall consist of a Senate and House of Representatives."

During the Nineteenth Century Chief Justice John Marshall had established the practice of judges legislating from the bench through the unconstitutional concept of *judicial review*,[22] and during the early years of the Twentieth Century Presidents Theodore Roosevelt and Woodrow Wilson perfected the practice of legislating through executive fiat – while, all along, claiming they were not usurping the U.S. Constitution.

The War to End All Wars (World War I) did not accomplish its aim of ending all wars. It did, however, create an opportunity for socialism to take a major leap forward. Woodrow Wilson took advantage of the opportunity created by The Great War to implement his own idealistic proposals for global governance. Progressive efforts in the United States expanded to a series of new collective efforts aimed at addressing worldwide problems that were believed to be beyond the capacity of individual nation-states to solve. While supporters of internationalism, such as Woodrow Wilson, claimed that the right of nations to self-determination would remain to be respected, the ultimate goal of many of those who sought a New World Order was a global governance system. They claimed that the loss of individual sovereignty of the various countries was for the purpose of the "global good". The early proposals led to the formation of international organizations such as the League of Nations, the United Nations, and the North Atlantic Treaty Organization (NATO). Other international organizations, such as the Bretton Woods system (1944-1971) and the General Agreement on Tariffs and Trade (GATT, 1947-1994) also emerged as a result of their collective drive for globalism.[23]

Progressives and socialists (the differences between the two are few and far between) embraced these new international organizations and regimes in the aftermath of the two World Wars, and worked to expand their scope of power in the hopes of spreading the political principles of collectivism worldwide.

Woodrow Wilson suffered a severe stroke October 2, 1919.[24] Even though at the Paris peace conference Wilson had persuaded the European Powers to adopt his Fourteen Points,[25] including establishment of a peace-keeping League of Nations, the U.S. Senate refused to ratify membership in it. After the stroke, Wilson served his remaining time in the presidency as an invalid,[26] relinquishing the Office of the Presidency to Warren Harding March 4, 1921. Wilson died only a few years later.

The end of the Wilson presidency also brought to a conclusion the Progressive Era. President Harding, a Republican, campaigned on a motto of a "return to normalcy." His successor, Calvin Coolidge, a strict constitutionalist, would lead America away from federal intrusion into the States, and into the most economically prosperous decade of her short history. The progressives, however, would return just in time to send the world into a Great Depression – which overwhelmed the nation – Within a few weeks after Black Thursday on the stock market, $30 billion of paper value, a sum larger than the national debt, had "vanished into thin air"…banks failed…by late 1932 and early 1933 industrial production had fallen by one half, construction by six sevenths, and farm prices, already depressed, by three fifths.[27] Manipulation of the currency by the federal reserve, ill-timed protectionist trade laws, and a return to federal intrusion into the States (largely through new social programs and public works programs) during the presidency of Herbert Hoover, and then through nearly four terms of Franklin Delano Roosevelt (Teddy's fifth-cousin), made sure the return to normalcy was short-lived – and that the next return would be delayed by at least seven years.[28]

Theodore Roosevelt passed away January 6, 1919. After cheating death his entire life, he died in his sleep at his Long Island estate. He was 60 years old, and had been undone by a coronary embolism.[29] Rumors have always swirled that say something along the line that Teddy Roosevelt verbalized regret for his progressive ways while on his death bed. The rumors have never been confirmed, and while the gesture would be a welcomed one, if it existed it came too late. Roosevelt, and his fellow progressives, had already done their damage.

DOUGLAS V. GIBBS

• 1: Alexander Hamilton

America today largely conforms to Alexander Hamilton's vision of what the United States could be someday in the future if led by an establishment of political elite. Hamilton, an important figure in the Revolutionary War, was a trusted companion of George Washington during the future President's time as Commander in Chief of the Continental Army. A patriot in the sense that he loved the United States of America, Hamilton envisioned the United States as being the next great empire, describing the fledgling country as being the "embryo of a great empire."[1] To achieve his vision, Hamilton believed, the political elite required much power and control over the country's internal and external affairs, placing him at odds with the concept of *laissez faire,* a style of non-intrusive government championed by his rival, Thomas Jefferson, and intended by most of the Founding Fathers during the writing of the United States Constitution.[2]

America was designed to be exceptional – an exception to the rule. The Founding Fathers purposely designed the American system of government to be nothing like what existed in Europe. The founders recognized the existence of the communist model, and feared it. It was not called communism, or socialism, back then. Samuel Adams called it a "Utopian scheme."[3]

Samuel Adams said, "The Utopian schemes of leveling (re-distribution of the wealth) and a community of goods (central ownership of the means of production and distribution), are as visionary and impractical as those which vest all property in the Crown. [These ideas] are arbitrary, despotic, and, in our government, unconstitutional."[4]

The Founding Fathers were aware of these big government concepts because they existed in Europe, and they existed in the minds of some of their own countrymen.

One of the European concepts that Alexander Hamilton bought into was that of "*The General Will*."

Prior to the French Revolution one of the heroes of the *Jacobins*, a group today that would be considered hardcore socialists, was a statist by the name of Jean-Jacques Rousseau. The philosophies of Rousseau were among the catalysts that brought about the French Revolution. As a supporter of big government, Rousseau championed the concept of *The General Will.*[5]

The General Will was designed to ensure the public good. *Nationalists* believed that the people were unable to properly maintain society. A central government power was required, according to their belief system, and a ruling elite was needed to ensure society ran smoothly, and operated in the best interest of the people. The political power was trusted by the people to serve The General Will, not their own individual interests.[6]

The propaganda behind The General Will convinced the people that the existence of The General Will was not only real, but existed in such a manner that it was not necessarily expressed by the general public. However, The General Will was presumed to be known only by the ruling elite. According to Rousseau, "no aspect of human life is excluded from the control of the general will," and "whosoever refuses to obey the general will must in that instance be restrained by the body politic, which actually means that he is forced to be free."[7]

Supporters of The General Will wished to dissolve the people into a homogeneous mass, abolish decentralization, and remove representative institutions. The Founding Fathers hated and feared the concept of The General Will, for if the concept were to invade the American System, then all voluntary associations would wind up becoming subjected to government regulation in the name of "the people," their "will," and for the "good of society." These mandates would be argued to be in The General Will, as interpreted by the ruling elite, and would enable the beginning of the end of individual liberty.[8]

Modern society exhibits examples of the government following the dictates of The General Will. Supporters of the concept of *Net Neutrality* claim that the internet cannot be free without government control. In other words, it must be forced to be free.

The leftist establishment states that the intrusion of government into our lives is necessary, and for the public interest. They believe that the "good of the community" ranks higher than the rights of the individual. These policies tend to benefit small, but powerful, special interests at the expense of the rest of the society, but are put into place by the ruling elite because the public doesn't understand any better, and must be forced to comply.

In New York City, a whole stack of intrusive laws have been constantly proposed, and a number of them have been implemented. "We've got to do something. Everybody is wringing their hands saying we've got to do something. Well, here is a concrete thing. You can still buy large bottles in stores. But in a restaurant, 16 ounces is the maximum that they would be able to serve in one cup. If you want to order two cups at the same time, that's fine. It's your choice. We're not taking away anybody's right to do things. We're simply forcing you to understand that you have to make the conscious decision to go from one cup to another cup," said NYC Mayor Michael Bloomberg about his proposal to ban sugary drinks 16oz or larger in 2012.[9]

Hamilton joined James Madison at the Annapolis Convention in 1786 in the call for a national convention to be held in Philadelphia the following May of 1787.[10] Disorderly elements of the new country had been raging to the point of a rebellion by the veterans of the Revolutionary War due to economic turmoil in the new country. Shays' Rebellion exposed the weaknesses of the government under the Articles of Confederation, which included the inability to form an army or quell domestic unrest. The recommendation was that a revision of the Articles was necessary. Only by revamping the Articles, it was argued, may America be able to properly address the challenges she was experiencing.[11]

George Washington had been urging such an action for years, for Washington and the Revolutionaries understood firsthand how the absence of a strongly unified command structure had indeed compromised America's military effectiveness in the fight against Britain.[12] The Annapolis Convention in 1786, while attended by only five States, had been organized specifically for the purpose of trying to figure out what to do regarding commerce. Among other issues, the States were in conflict over waterways. In an effort to encourage free commerce between the States, as well as providing greater opportunity for the transportation of goods, a commission in 1785 declared that the Potomac project would create an open waterway for both Maryland and Virginia, as well as for all of the States.[13] George Washington hoped the project would open up trade between the States along the northern Atlantic Coast with the frontier emerging in the regions near the Ohio River.[14] Few debates between the States were fiercer than those which addressed commerce between them.

Hamilton was a fierce negotiator and instinctively hurled himself at opposition when it arose. When it came to his perceived need for a more centralized government, he never stopped his drive and push for a convention. The States would not listen, and it was only by persistence and skilled maneuvering of a few men, including Hamilton, did the Federal Convention meet at all.[15] He imposed his personality upon the issues he believed in, convincingly debating with a take-charge attitude that few were able to defend against.

As a defender of the U.S. Constitution, and someone who urged the States to ratify the document, he was one of the three authors of the Federalist Essays to the State of New York, contributing to 51 of the 85 papers.[16] He had called for the national convention during the Annapolis Convention, and he was a champion for the Constitution's ratification, even though he felt that the United States Constitution did not go far enough in establishing a new, more powerful, centralized government.

In reality, Hamilton's core political and economic ideas were not in line with what the majority of the Founding Fathers intended when they constructed the U.S. Constitution. His intellectual, legal and political battles would create consequences that America continues to suffer from more than two centuries later. His America was one of collectivism and currency manipulation, rather than free enterprise and individual liberty. He claimed to be a defender of the Constitution, when in reality his ambition was to usurp it and establish an America that was more like a dictatorial monarchy, using centralized power and economic mercantilism to create an empire that rivaled, and hopefully would surpass, the reach of the British Empire.

Hamilton was the first Treasury Secretary of the United States. He was a skilled lawyer, founder of the New York Post newspaper, and the founder of the Bank of New York. He was an aristocratic New Yorker who was egomaniacal, and had a "feverish, sometimes even grotesque concern for his reputation. Fame . . . was the spur of this remarkable man."[17]

Thomas Jefferson viewed Hamilton as being a deadly threat to American liberty. He accused

Hamilton of pursuing "imperial glory" (and glory for himself). Hamilton was a relentless statist who was "always and everywhere working to expand the size and scope of government."[18]

Hamilton's love of government served as a constant motive for his political activities. He viewed the Constitution not through a lens of limited government, but as an instrument that could legitimize virtually any act of government if proper interpretation was provided by well-placed clever lawyers and judges. However, when Jefferson won the presidency in 1800, Hamilton turned against the document, calling it "a frail and worthless fabric."[19]

On the economic front, Hamilton considered a perpetual national debt, "if it is not excessive…a public blessing." The voluntary union of States would likely survive any threats of secession, argued Hamilton, because the States were tied to the burden of debt.[20]

During the presidency of John Adams, Hamilton's Federalist Party increased federal spending dramatically, which, in turn, led to an increase in taxation and governmental borrowing. The national debt soared to a total of over $80 million, a debt that required 80% of the annual expenditures to service it, and consumed over 40% of the tax revenue. Hamilton's irresponsible economic policies followed a period where the fledgling country had been tottering on the brink of bankruptcy.[21] Jefferson, during his presidency, worked to reduce the debt, reducing it by $25 million by 1807. The debt rose again during the Madison administration as a result of the War of 1812, but was again reduced, this time by $58 million, by Presidents James Monroe and John Quincy Adams. Andrew Jackson ran his campaign on the promise of eliminating the national debt, and the existence of the Bank of the United States. He succeeded in fulfilling both campaign promises. On January 1, 1835, President Jackson announced that the federal government was "free from public debt.[22]

William Graham Sumner later explained, during the late 1800s, regarding Hamilton's central banking philosophies, "A national bank...was not essential to the work of the federal government...This was...only a measure for carrying out the...interweaving of the interests of wealthy men with those of the government."[23]

Hamilton was, among other things, also the founding father of Crony Capitalism and Corporate Welfare. In addition to a government-directed economy, Hamilton made it clear that it was his opinion that the government should work with massive corporations, and use government influences to benefit politically connected businesses. At the time, the practice was called "mercantilism." Hamilton maintained that government intervention was necessary, and that if the government did not provide tax-financed subsidies for businesses, manufacturing would never develop. In his *Report on Manufactures* Hamilton argued for using government to try to make certain manufacturing industries appear earlier than they otherwise would on the free market[24] – a practice that is followed today by the Democrat Party, of which they are trying to apply to "renewable resources" industries.

While Hamilton wrote in defense of the United States Constitution in his essays of the Federalist Papers, it was Hamilton who began the practice of constitutional "interpretation," and "implied law." To defend his idea of the Bank of the United States, Hamilton used his own definitions of the General Welfare Clause and the "Necessary and Proper" Clause (referred to by progressives as the "Elastic Clause"). He claimed the General Welfare Clause was a license for the Congress to do anything it pleased as long as it was considered for the welfare of the republic. When Jefferson argued the proposed central bank was not "necessary," and therefore was unconstitutional, Hamilton argued that Jefferson did not know what the word "necessary" means. *Definitions of words, reasoned Hamilton, was a matter of opinion.* Hamilton explained that the federal government's powers ought to be based "on principles of liberal construction," and for the "advancement of the public good." The ruling class, as guardians of the public good, must use "great latitude of discretion" when deciding how to legislate – even if it meant fabricating constitutional authority in order to grant a power to Congress.[25]

Hamilton's teachings led to a concept later championed by Teddy Roosevelt and Woodrow Wilson more than a hundred years later, that, "any act by the government is constitutional, as long as it is not expressly prohibited by the Constitution."[26] The notion was foreign to the delegates on the floor of the Constitutional Convention in 1787, because such an idea was never discussed, nor intended. The purpose of the limiting principles in the Constitution were to bind down and restrain the federal government, not give it unfettered power over everything based on the idea that it's for the public good.

According to Hamilton, the federal government has "implied powers,"[27] which are powers shaped and twisted to fit constitutional definitions by clever politicians and judges, even though they are not expressly enumerated in the Constitution.

Hamilton used his "implied powers" argument to establish the Bank of the United States in 1791. Once in place, Hamilton's central bank created inflation by overprinting massive amounts of currency.[28]

"Hamilton had no equal among the men who chose to interpret the Constitution as a reservoir of national energy."[29] The practice of reading things in the Constitution that were not really there continued after Hamilton was killed as the result of a dual with

Aaron Burr.

The principles of constitutional subversion, thanks to Hamilton, eventually spread throughout the judicial branch once the Federalist Party faithfully retreated to the courts after Jefferson's electoral win in 1800. Or, as Jefferson put it, "The principal of them [meaning: the leaders of the political opposition] have retreated into the judiciary as a stronghold, the tenure of which renders it difficult to dislodge them."[30] By the 1830s the courts had fortified the concept of federal supremacy, while chipping away at State sovereignty and voluntary membership in the union.

As a result of Hamilton's constitutional lies, the branches of government have been flipped. Originally, the voice of the people through the House of Representatives carried the strongest torch in government, followed by the voice of the States through the Senate, the executive branch, and lastly the judicial branch. In fact, John Jay turned down the opportunity to return to his post as Chief Justice specifically because of the weak position of the court system in American Society.

John Jay, the first Chief Justice of the United States, resigned his post to become the governor of the State of New York. After his term as governor ended, during which time two other persons had held the chief post on the United States Supreme Court, John Adams asked John Jay if he would serve as Chief

Justice again. Adams had just lost the latest presidential election, and his big government Federalist Party had lost both Houses of Congress. To preserve some vestige of statism in the U.S. Government, Adams began appointing "midnight judges."

Jay turned Adams down, complaining that the Court lacked "energy, weight, and dignity which are essential to its affording due support to the national government." He added, "Hence I am induced to doubt both the propriety and the expediency of my returning to the bench under the present system."[31]

In other words, the fact that the Judicial Branch was the weakest of the three branches made it not worth holding a position, according to Jay. However, he ended his comment with the words "under the present system," which means he was a believer that in the future the court would expand its power.

During Hamilton's living years, however, Jefferson's concept of *laissez faire* prevailed. Hamilton's economic and political agenda was defeated over and over again. While the Hamiltonian ideas began to grow in strength in the courts, it wasn't until nearly a century after the Shot Heard 'Round the World that Hamilton's statism finally made it into the White House in a big way. After the War Between the States, the concept of voluntary membership in the union of States was replaced by a new blueprint for America, which included mandatory membership, federal supremacy, and a political hegemony in Washington that to this day exists. Economic interventionism has become the norm. Interpretation of the Constitution through the lens of implied law is taught in the law schools and is practiced in the world of law. Corporate welfare runs amok, and our country is ruled by a judicial dictatorship.

As for the progressives who champion Hamiltonian politics, they love Alexander Hamilton so much that they created a musical worshipping the man, which did quite well on Broadway.

• 2: John Marshall

 **W**hen John Jay turned down the opportunity to return as Chief Justice of the United States, he complained that the Supreme Court was too limited in its powers. The judges were only authorized to apply the law to the cases they heard, but if they believed any law to be unfair, unjust, or unconstitutional, they could only provide an opinion. Due to the concept of Separation of Powers, only Congress could create, modify, or strike-down any laws the judges reviewed as not consistent with the Constitution.

John Adams, after Jay rejected his offer, turned to John Marshall. Marshall accepted, and for more than thirty years he molded the Supreme Court into a primary force. The federal court system, under the iron rule of John Marshall, acquired the power of judicial review, and became a powerful and feared branch of the central government.

In today's American Society there is no question in

the minds of the average citizen that the judges are the final arbiters of constitutional authority. Through their stolen power, the courts have altered the Constitution into an instrument of the legal system elite, not of the States and We the People as originally intended.

Marshall, a student of Hamilton, expanded the latter's philosophy of implied powers, and he used judicial rulings and judicial opinion to strengthen the federal government by granting to it through judicial fiat more authorities on the basis of federal supremacy.

In the months following the signing of the U.S. Constitution in Philadelphia, John Marshall became a fierce defender of the Constitution during the Virginia Ratification Convention. It was Marshall who made the proposal calling for a ratification convention, and when in October of 1787 the House of Delegates passed Marshall's proposal, "both sides immediately began jockeying for position. The newspapers filled with articles pro and con; prospective delegates began to issue personal manifestos; and in New York, Madison, Hamilton, and John Jay commenced publication of their remarkable essays defending and explaining the Constitution, *The Federalist* papers. As a counterpoise to the nationalist drumbeat, George Mason issued his *Objections to the Constitution*; Richard Henry Lee published what is generally regarded as the most incisive critique of national power, *Letters from the Federal Farmer*; and Patrick Henry kept up a steady fusillade against the proposed Constitution in public meetings throughout Virginia."[1]

Virginia served as a primary focus of the constitutional debate. The State had one-fifth of the overall population of the new country, and over one-third of the union's commerce.[2]

James Madison, in order to quell the fears of those who believed the Constitution granted the federal government too much national power, pointed towards the States as a countervailing authority. Arguments during the Virginia Ratification Convention against the Constitution, presented largely by Patrick Henry and George Mason, were very persuasive, and the federalists realized they needed to neutralize Henry and Mason. They revised their strategy, and put John Marshall up front to speak for the constitutionalists. The anti-federalists countered with James Monroe.

"Monroe versus Marshall. The schoolboy chums, wartime friends, and political and personal companions were now squaring off in debate. Monroe, like Madison, was poor at public speaking and was selected by the antifederalists because of his military background. Thus far, no officer from Wasington's army had spoken against the Constitution, and the antifederalists needed to demonstrate their patriotism…Monroe was known to be a protégé of Jefferson…each side sought to invoke Jefferson's support."[3]

Marshall's remarks during the convention gives us a clue to his views of the Constitution. Like Hamilton, Marshall was disappointed that the Constitution did not create a powerful centralized government, but he saw it as a step in the right direction when compared to the Articles of Confederation. He approached the document as a lawyer, rather than a statesman, stressing the need for experienced men to handle matters of governance so that they may recognize any "inconveniences," and then "embark on attempts to correct it."[4]

"What are objects of the national government?" asked Marshall.[5]

As Chief Justice of the United States, Marshall's contempt for the limitations upon the central government became obvious. He worked feverishly to advance the concept of federal supremacy and national power. In his opinion regarding the *McCullough v. Maryland* case, Marshall wrote, "Let the end be legitimate, let it be within the scope of the Constitution, and all means which are appropriate, which are plainly adapted to that end, which are not prohibited, but consistent with the letter and the spirit of the Constitution, are constitutional."[6]

In short, if the power is deemed necessary, then it exists.

Marshall rarely relied on information related to the original intent of the Constitution. He did not refer to any notes taken during the convention, nor on the State ratification conventions, in his constitutional interpretations. He mostly cited Hamilton's entries into the Federalist Papers, clinging to Hamilton's nationalist views, a viewpoint rejected by the convention of 1787. During his thirty-five year stint as Chief Justice, he worked diligently to replace the original intent of the Constitution with "constitutional law," which consists of judicial opinions, case law, and precedent. It was Marshall's goal to alter the American Form of Government from Jeffersonian limited government and federalism to Hamiltonian nationalism, placing the interpretation of the Constitution in the hands of five government lawyers with lifetime tenure.

Virginian St. George Tucker recognized what was happening, and wrote in his book *View of the Constitution of the United States*, that if "unlimited authority" of the central government were ever to extend so far as to change the Constitution itself through judicial fiat, then "the government, whatever be its form," would become "absolute and despotic."[7]

John Taylor, in his book *Tyranny Unmasked*, agreed. He wrote that the Constitution as "an essential principle for preserving liberty…never could have designed to destroy it, by investing five or six men, installed for life, with a power of regulating the constitutional rights of all political departments."[8]

Marshall's campaign to alter the American System of Government began early. In *Marbury v. Madison* (1803), through his written opinion, Marshal established *judicial review* – the power of the federal court system to examine law (and eventually the activities of the President were added) and determine if the law in question may be struck down due to it being unjust, or unconstitutional, in the opinion of the courts.[9]

Marshall wrote, "The powers of the Legislature are defined and limited; and [so] that those limits may not be mistaken or forgotten, the Constitution is written...the very essence of judicial duty [is to follow the Constitution]...It is emphatically the province and duty of the judicial department to say what the law is...a law repugnant to the Constitution is void, and courts as well as other departments, are bound by that instrument."[10]

In the instance of federal laws, that means that the federal government, through the court system, may determine its own authorities – essentially creating a judicial tyranny where legal oligarchs may overthrow the legislative achievements of the representatives of the people in the name of interpretation.

By placing the judges above the legislative branch

and the States, with power over all legislation, Marshall established that unelected judges who never have to face the public through election, therefore making them immune to public criticism, would be the ones tasked with making all constitutional decisions in relation to what the Constitution really meant, and how it could be defined.

The goal was to establish the federal government as supreme over the States, and to use the judicial branch as the authority declaring so. To make sure the superiority of the judicial branch survived any legislative opposition, Marshall asserted that he, as chief justice, had power over all congressional legislation. His assertion was established as part of Alexander Hamilton's "expansive" view of the Constitution, reinterpreting the document in such a way as to expand the powers and scope of the federal government as much as possible. He aimed to establish a new Supreme Court function – to establish an uncontestable power to say what the law is.

Thomas Jefferson spoke out against what Marshall was up to. In a September 6, 1819 letter to Judge Spencer Roane, he wrote, "My construction of the constitution is…that each department [i.e., branch of government] is truly independent of the others, and has an equal right to decide for itself what is the meaning of the constitution in the cases submitted to its action".[11]

By the dawn of the War Between the States the power of the federal court system to determine the constitutionality of federal legislation was in full swing. By the end of the war, federal supremacy through the courts was no longer challenged.

Woodrow Wilson later wrote, "The War between the States established...this principle, that the federal government is, through the courts, the final judge of its own powers."[12]

John Marshall used a series of rulings to establish the judicial branch as the unquestioned authority over the Constitution, the legislative and executive branches, the States, and We the People.

- *Marbury v. Madison (1803), Judicial Review*

  John Marshall: "It is emphatically the province and duty of the Judicial Department to say what the law is. Those who apply the rule to particular cases must, of necessity, expound and interpret that rule. If two laws conflict with each other, the Courts must decide on the operation of each...Certainly all those who have framed written constitutions contemplate them as forming the fundamental and paramount law of the nation, and consequently the theory of every such government must be, that an act of the legislature repugnant to the Constitution is void."[13]

Note: *Marbury v. Madison* was also the first and only case in which the Marshall Court ruled an act of Congress unconstitutional,[14] and thereby reinforced the doctrine of Judicial Review.

The impact was that Marshall's opinion set in motion a series of rulings and political maneuvers to unconstitutionally alter the chain of command among the branches of government, the States, and We the People. While the original intent of the U.S. Constitution was to establish the legislative branch as the strongest of the three branches, and to relegate the judicial branch to applying the law to the cases they heard, and only giving opinion when they believed there were questions regarding the constitutionality of a law, Marshall had flipped the table, launching not only a campaign to establish federal supremacy over the States, but judicial supremacy over the other branches of government.

- *United States v. Peters* (1809), States could neither annul the judgments nor determine the jurisdiction of federal courts. Pennsylvania claimed the federal government had no right, based on the 11th Amendment, to sue the State. John Marshall's Supreme Court argued that the high court could not only strike down a State statute, but that the States' legislatures must bend to the dictates of the federal courts.

"If the legislatures of the several States may, at will, annul the judgments of the courts of the United States, and destroy the rights acquired under those judgments," wrote Justice Marshall, "the Constitution itself becomes a solemn mockery, and the nation is deprived of the means of enforcing its laws by the instrumentality of its own tribunals."[15]

The case began during the Revolutionary War. Gideon Olmstead, a Connecticut sea captain who had been captured by the British during the Revolutionary War, and then was forced to serve on a British ship as part of its crew, worked with others in the same predicament to overcome the British crew and steer the ship towards New Jersey. In the process, a ship belonging to Pennsylvania intercepted the British sloop and brought it to port in Philadelphia. The captain of *the Convention*, the ship belonging to Pennsylvania, claimed the British vessel as being his prize. The Connecticut sailors who had taken over the ship and were steering it towards New Jersey before *the Convention* intercepted it disagreed. The dispute wound up in Pennsylvania's admiralty court. Pennsylvania's Court of Admiralty decided that any proceeds from the sale of the Active would be divided between the Commonwealth of Pennsylvania, which owned the Convention, and the officers and men of the three vessels involved. Under this arrangement, Olmstead and his shipmates would receive only one quarter of the total value of the sloop.[16]

Olmstead and his fellows filed an appeal which went in their favor in 1778. However, Court of Admiralty Judge George Ross refused to honor the appeal court's verdict. Judge Ross ordered the British ship to be sold, and Olmstead quickly got an injunction ordering the marshall in charge of the sale to deliver the proceeds to the appeals court. The marshall ignored the order and delivered the money to Judge Ross. Olmstead and gang then filed suit against Judge Ross, who had at this point had the sale proceeds transformed into U.S. loan certificates. The certificates were then turned over to David Rittenhouse, a prominent Philadelphian who was the State of Pennsylvania's treasurer. Rittenhouse in turn gave Judge Ross a certificate of indemnity against any future claims upon the sum.

Rittenhouse never got around to handing the loan certificates over to the State of Pennsylvania, so they remained in his personal account accruing interest until he died. After Rittenhouse's death, Olmstead and the other claimants brought suit against Elizabeth Serjeant and Esther Waters, the executrixes of the Rittenhouse estate, demanding that the money be turned over in accordance with the court of appeals decision. Pennsylvania's

General Assembly finally became interested in the money and passed a legislative act in 1801 demanding that Rittenhouse's estate deliver the certificates to the State treasury. With the State of Pennsylvania using legislation to claim the certificates, and an appeals judge claiming the certificates belonged to Olmstead, both claiming the certificates, the executrixes decided to give the certificates to nobody.[17]

The uncertainty continued until 1808, when Olmstead and gang attempted to get Philadelphia U.S. District Court Judge Richard Peters to grant an attachment against the Rittenhouse estate. When Peters refused, Olmstead succeeded in obtaining a writ of mandamus, an order to carry out the higher federal appeals court's decision that had ruled in favor of Olmstead. Peters stated that he would decline to order the certificates to change hands as long as the State of Pennsylvania, through its piece of legislation, was still involved as a claimant. Judge Peters then cited the 11th Amendment to the Constitution, which prevents the judicial power of the United States from extending to any lawsuit prosecuted against any of the individual states. Since Rittenhouse had been Pennsylvania's treasurer, Peters ruled, the State could claim jurisdiction over the case.[18]

Meanwhile, the State of Pennsylvania was threatening to use armed force to prevent the appeals court sentence from being carried out. Faced with the state militia on one side and a federal writ on the other, Judge Peters returned the mandamus to the U.S. Supreme Court and waited for a decision.

Which brings us to the court's 1809 decision that commanded Judge Peters to act on the mandamus. Chief Justice Marshall pointed out that the disputed certificates had never been the actual property of the State of Pennsylvania. They had always been in the possession of David Rittenhouse or his estate. Since Rittenhouse had always acted as a private citizen in the affair, the 11th Amendment prohibition against making a State a party in a lawsuit was not an issue.[19]

The U.S. Supreme Court repudiated the contention that the Pennsylvania legislature's 1801 act demanding the money was legally superior to the federal appeals court decision.

"If the legislatures of the several States may, at will, annul the judgements of the courts of the United States, and destroy the rights acquired under those judgements," wrote Justice Marshall, "the Constitution itself becomes a solemn mockery, and the nation is deprived of the means of enforcing its laws by the instrumentality of its own tribunals."[20]

The Supreme Court declared that States could

neither annul the judgments nor determine the jurisdiction of federal courts. Since the court of appeals in the active case had been formed by the Continental Congress, its decision superseded Pennsylvania's Court of Admiralty. Judge Peters was ordered to act on the mandamus, while making sure that the executrixes of the Rittenhouse estate were protected from any possible legal repercussions.[21]

The Court's decision established "national law," strengthening the power of the federal courts while delegitimatizing the concept that the States were the parents over their creation, the federal government.

- *Fletcher v. Peck* (1810). This ruling served as being the first time the federal courts struck down a State law as unconstitutional.[22] The case became a precedent for all other cases against the States. The move was a direct assault on State Sovereignty and established a starting point for allowing the federal government to dictate to the States what they can and cannot do even if the issue is strictly only a State authority. A little more than fifty years later (after the War Between the States), with the 14th Amendment, the concept of allowing the federal government to dictate control over the States, even regarding issues not authorized to the federal government, was reinforced in the world of case law by the

Equal Protection Clause and the Due Process Clause.

The case began in 1795 when the Georgia State legislature granted roughly 35 million acres of state land to the Yazoo Land Companies for the rate of 1.5 cents per acre. It was later discovered that the deal was shrouded by corruption, and all but one legislator had been bribed. In 1796, a new State legislature repealed the corrupt land grant. In 1800, John Peck bought some of the land that was part of the 1795 grant, and sold 13,000 acres of it to Robert Fletcher in 1803. When Fletcher discovered that the sale of the land had been voided by State law, he sued Peck, hoping to get damages, on the grounds that Peck had lied to him as to the status of the land. A federal circuit court ruled in favor of Peck, but Fletcher appealed to the Supreme Court. The question left for the court to answer was whether or not the act of 1796 (repealing the act of 1795) was a violation of Article 1, Section 10 of the Constitution.[23]

The Marshall Court decided that the sale was in violation of the Contract Clause of the Constitution (Article 1, Section 10) which forbids States from, "passing any Law impairing the obligation of contracts". According to Marshall and his U.S. Supreme Court, the act of the Georgia legislature rescinding a land grant was unconstitutional because it revoked the rights previously granted by the contract.[24]

- *Martin v. Hunter's Lessee* (1816). This ruling served as an important cog in establishing the statist concept of a court hierarchy, which states that the municipal, county and State courts are simply rungs on a hierarchical ladder, which continues upwards through the federal court system, and ultimately to the United States Supreme Court, making the Supreme Court the highest court in the land. Marshall took no part in the consideration or decision of the case, recusing himself citing a financial conflict of interest. Nonetheless, his team by 1816 was fully set and they understood and largely abided by Marshall's agenda. The case ultimately established Federal Supremacy in Civil Cases. The case was regarding a State law in Virginia which allowed the State to confiscate the property of a loyalist. The Virginia State supreme court upheld the confiscation, claiming that the argument that a treaty overruled the State's law was invalid based on its own interpretation of the treaty, the treaty did not cover the dispute. The U.S. Supreme Court then remanded the case back to the Virginia court, which then decided the U.S. Supreme Court did not have authority over cases originating in State court. The U.S. Supreme Court then reversed the State court's decision on appeal, and ruled that any questions regarding federal law, even if in the jurisdiction of a State, are within the jurisdiction of the federal courts; thus, establishing further federal court supremacy in matters of constitutional interpretation. A part of the argument provided by Virginia was that federal judicial power came from the States, therefore the U.S. Supreme Court, nor any other federal court, had the authority to overrule a State's interpretation of a treaty, or the Constitution, without its consent. Joseph Story argued that the power was not granted by the States, but by the people democratically, therefore the Supremacy Clause applies, allowing the Supreme Court's interpretation to trump the State's interpretation.[25] Story's argument not only advanced the concept of federal supremacy, but also aided in promoting the fallacy that the United States is a democracy.

- *Dartmouth College v. Woodward* (1819). Ultimately, this ruling limited State authorities regarding corporations and corporate charters. The case revolved around contracts and government involvement as it relates to institutions older than the still-young union of States. Dartmouth College's history reaches back to a charter from King George III of England in 1769. A charter is a type of contract, outlining the rights and responsibilities of the institution being created. This charter established Dartmouth College, outlined its purpose and structure, and established that it was to be a private, not public, school of higher education.[26]

In 1816, the State government of New Hampshire decided that Dartmouth should be a public school and rewrote the school's charter. The new charter also changed how the trustees of the school were selected and what their powers entailed.[27]

The existing trustees were not in favor of the changes to the charter made by the State government, claiming New Hampshire was overstepping its legal authority by interfering with the contract of a private institution. The former trustees hired New Hampshire statesman Daniel Webster as their lawyer, and filed a lawsuit against William Woodward, the State-appointed secretary of the board of Dartmouth under the new charter. The case made its way to the Supreme Court in 1819.[28]

The Supreme Court ruled 5-1 in favor of the former trustees, finding that the new charter was invalid because Article 1, Section 10 of the United States Constitution prohibits States from impairing, weakening, or canceling a contract. The charter that established Dartmouth was a contract, so the State of New Hampshire could not revise it. The fact that the contract dated to while New Hampshire was still a colony of England or that Dartmouth was established before the Constitution was written did not influence the decision.[29]

While the ruling was accurate from a constitutional point of view, the ruling and written opinion by John Marshall established that the federal courts would be the final arbiters regarding all cases involving contracts. The voices of the States were essentially cut off from being involved in any case in which a contract was the issue, and the case gave the federal government yet another way into involving itself in internal issues of which the Constitution never authorized.[30]

- *McCulloch v. Maryland* (1819). This was the case that gave Alexander Hamilton's idea of implied powers a nice big set of judicial choppers. In their ruling regarding *McCulloch v. Maryland,* the Supreme Court held that Congress has implied powers derived from those listed in Article I, Section 8.[31] The "Necessary and Proper" Clause was applied as being the constitutional authority allowing the concept of implied powers, which is the same argument Hamilton used to convince his contemporaries that Congress had the power to establish a national bank.

The second National Bank of the United States was established in 1816. Many States opposed branches of the National Bank within their borders. They did not want the National Bank competing with their own banks, and objected to the establishment of a National Bank as an unconstitutional exercise of Congress's power.[32]

To discourage the establishment of the National Bank inside her borders, the State of Maryland imposed a tax on the bank of $15,000 per year. Cashier James McCulloch of the Baltimore branch refused to pay the amount and sued. The case went to the Supreme Court with Maryland arguing that as a sovereign State, it had the power to tax any business within its borders. McCulloch's attorneys argued that a national bank was "necessary and proper" for Congress to establish in order to carry out its enumerated powers.[33]

Chief Justice Marshall wrote, "Although, among the enumerated powers of government, we do not find the word 'bank,'...we find the great powers to lay and collect taxes; to borrow money; to regulate commerce...Let the end be legitimate, let it be within the scope of the constitution, and all means which are appropriate, which are plainly adapted to that end, which are not prohibited, but consist with the letter and spirit of the constitution, are constitutional."[34]

The Marshall Court ruled against Maryland taxing the national bank, "That the power to tax involves the power to destroy. . . . If the states may tax one instrument, employed by the [federal] government in the execution of its powers, they may tax any and every other instrument….This was not intended by the American people. They did not design to make their government dependent on the states."[35]

Marshall also noted an important difference between the Constitution and the Articles of Confederation (the United States' first governing document that had been replaced by the Constitution). The Articles said that the States retained all powers not "expressly" given to the federal government. The 10th Amendment, Marshall noted, did not include the word "expressly." This was further evidence, he argued, that the Constitution did not limit Congress to doing only those things specifically listed in Article I.[36]

James Madison's essay, Federalist #45, which explains that the powers of the federal government are "few and defined" was never even uttered by Marshall. As with all Hamiltonians, Marshall disagreed with the concept that it was the States who created the federal government, making them the parents over the central government.

- *Cohens v. Virginia* (1821). The *Cohens* ruling demolished all claims of State Sovereignty or States' Rights. In the words of Marshall, the case "decide[d] all cases of every description under the laws of the United States...The Constitution and laws of a state, insofar as they are repugnant to the Constitution and laws of the United States are absolutely void."[37]

The case was an appeal, brought by two highly paid lawyers, on behalf of two speculators hoping to reap a multi-state harvest from a District of Columbia lottery.

Marshall unequivocally asserted the "We, the People" with which the Constitution began meant the Union, Congress and the Supreme Court created by that Constitution reigned over the States because it was created by the people, rather than the States. He dismissed the union, referring to the United States in a national sense. If the country is a single nation, and one people, he argued, then we must be one in all federal regulations, as well.

"It is their government, and in that character they have no other," Marshall declared. "America has chosen to be a...nation; and for all these purposes, her government is complete...it is competent...it is supreme."[38]

The United States was never intended to be a nation. It is a federation of States. To Marshall, the States are nothing more than provinces created to be subservient to the supremacy of the federal government. In the eyes of Marshall, who was in full agreement with the claims of the Cohens' lawyers, Virginia had no authority to impose any fines or fees as a sovereign State because a "sovereign state, independent of the Union," does not exist. Otherwise, "the Union [is] a mere league or confederacy," argued William Pinckney, another Cohens' attorney and the nation's highest paid lawyer.[39]

By the end of it all, States' rights advocates were enraged and suspicious, knowing that Marshall had used the case to assert the supremacy of the Union over the States.

- *Gibbons v. Ogden* (1824). This ruling was the first to challenge and rewrite the original intent of the Commerce Clause.[40] The Commerce Clause, when it comes to interstate commerce, was originally intended to only be in play when there is a dispute between the States. The gross misrepresentation we believe to be the law of the land today, which places the federal government in complete authority to control and restrict commerce by rule of law, was first fueled by John Marshall.

During the early years of the fledgling United States, the States acted as bitter rivals when it came to commerce. During the discussion between the delegates in the Constitutional Convention on August 29, 1787,[41] it was acknowledged that the New England States desired strong regulations regarding commerce. Meanwhile, the Southern States were calling for no federal regulatory powers over interstate commerce. The remaining States carried various opinions that may be considered to be quite moderate in relation to the other opinions. It was agreed that no State should be able to charge any taxes regarding import or export to or with other States or with other countries (Article I, Section 10 of the U.S. Constitution), and thanks to George Mason's efforts on September 15th in Convention, the Commerce Clause was not written with the intent to give the federal government a general controlling power over interstate commerce, either.

The concern regarding commerce between the States, during the time of the Constitutional Convention, was more about better enabling the flow of commerce between the States, not placing restrictions. The rivalry between the States regarding trade was already creating a restrictive environment, when it came to commerce between the States, so the need was for the new federal government to have a tool to better enable a free flow of commerce between the States.[42]

James Madison, in a letter to Joseph C. Cabell on September 18, 1828 explains that the Commerce Clause was not designed to restrict trade, but to encourage it. To encourage trade between the States, the federal government's involvement must be as limited as possible. The clause was to also encourage manufacturing, while restricting the federal government from showing preferential treatment towards any manufacturer. While in British Common Law, regulating trade means to tax it, in his letter Madison specifically explains, "a power to regulate trade does not involve a power to tax it." Commerce was also specifically defined as trade of goods or products between people or business entities, and did not include the manufacturing of products.[43]

Furthermore, the definition of the word "regulate" is also an important factor in determining what was originally intended. During the decades following the Constitution, those who defended the original intent of the Commerce Clause claimed that "regulate" means "to make regular."

When we consult the period's spellers, which were later organized into a dictionary, the 1828 Webster's Dictionary, we find that among the most common usages of the word "regulate" was, "To put in good order; as, to regulate the disordered state of a nation or its finances."[44]

Taking this information into the context of the Commerce Clause, this is what we must deduce from it. First, to put in good order the disordered condition of trade between the States in the United States at the time of the writing of the U.S. Constitution was more paramount than allowing the federal government to use rules or restrictions that may limit trade. What was most important to the framers of the Constitution was ensuring that commerce in a general sense was "in good order," since the current state of commerce both between the States, and with foreign countries, was in a disordered condition. To enable commerce to be in good order, that would mean that the federal government's intrusion into interstate commerce would need to be as limited as possible, only allowing Congress to make legislation when necessary to put interstate commerce in good order when an occurrence arises that may inhibit such trade between the States. These Congressional "rules" would be for the purpose of encouraging trade, not restricting it.

The necessity was to enable the free flow of commerce, rather than putting in place restrictive regulations. The federal government needed to be allowed to disallow the States from creating a hostile environment when it came to interstate commerce, while at the same time to not be allowed to impose its own restrictive rules that may interfere with interstate commerce. Therefore, federal intrusion by the federal government was prohibited, unless there was a conflict between the States, at which time the federal government may get involved in order to act as a mediator.

Gibbons v. Ogden, or the "Steamboat Case," was decided in the year 1824.[45] The background of the case was regarding a grant to Livingston and Fulton of an exclusive privilege to operate steamboats on the waters of the state of New York during a fixed number of years. Ogden was the assignee of that privilege. Gibbons operated a steamboat between a New Jersey port and New York, and he held a federal coasting license for his vessel under the act of Congress providing for the licensing of coastal vessels. Ogden applied for and obtained an injunction against Gibbons in the New York courts,' and the case eventually came up on error to the Supreme Court. The question before the Court was whether the commerce clause invalidated the act of a State purporting to grant an exclusive right to navigate the waters of that State. The case was a critical one because several states - New Jersey, Connecticut, and Ohio - had passed retaliatory statutes excluding from their waters any vessel licensed under the Fulton-Livingston monopoly.[46]

However, a larger political issue emerged. It turned out that the meaning of the term "commerce" as used in the commerce clause, was in question – specifically, whether it included "navigation." Although it was contended by counsel for Ogden that "commerce" meant merely "buying and selling," Marshall held that the power to regulate navigation was "as expressly granted, as if that term had been added to the word 'commerce'". And, he also stated that "commerce" not only comprehended every species of commercial intercourse among States and nation, but the power to prescribe rules for carrying on that intercourse.[47]

Marshall also held that, under the commerce clause, an act of Congress dealing with the subject matter of the clause is superior to a State statute inconsistent therewith and dealing with the same subject matter.[48]

After all of the dust settled, the move to apply federal supremacy to the commerce clause was in full swing. Marshall's vision for the commerce clause came to tyrannical fruition in 1942, with the *Wickard v. Filburn* case. *Wickard v. Filburn* led to an interpretation of the commerce clause indicating that intrastate economic activity "affects" interstate commerce. In other words, by goods not crossing State lines, it affects interstate commerce by reducing the number of goods that could have crossed state lines.[49]

Wickard grew wheat for his own family's consumption, but the U.S. Supreme Court reasoned that the wheat being consumed locally would keep wheat that was once sold across State lines from being sold in interstate commerce. By withdrawing that wheat from the interstate market, output and prices in interstate commerce were affected, therefore giving the federal government the authority to regulate it, and tax it.[50]

The *Wickard v. Filburn* case set the precedent that is now used in all cases regarding interstate commerce, and convinced an entire nation that despite the original intent of the U.S. Constitution, the federal government has the unbridled authority to regulate commerce between the States any way it chooses.

- *Worcester v. Georgia* (1832) was the last of three cases regarding indigenous American tribes (also *Johnson v. M'Intosh* (1823), *Cherokee Nation v. Georgia* (1831)) which established Federal Supremacy over Tribal Affairs.[51]

Prior to this case *the States* established, through legislation, what lands were considered to belong to the various Indian Tribes throughout the country. At this time, while the Native American groups were considered to be separate sovereign nations, the lands they resided upon still belonged to the States.

Samuel Worcester was indicted in a superior court in Georgia "for residing on the 15th of

July, 1831, in that part of the Cherokee Nation attached by the laws of the State of Georgia, without license or permit, and without having taken the oath to support and defend the constitution and laws of the State of Georgia, etc."[52]

Worcester claimed that he was a citizen of Vermont who had entered the Cherokee Nation as a missionary under the authority of the President of the United States and with permission of the Cherokee Nation. He had been given the permission with the understanding that his presence on Cherokee lands would be for the purpose of preaching The Gospel. He argued that Georgia had no jurisdiction over the matter because the United States recognized the Cherokee Nation as a sovereign nation, and proof of that is that the U.S. made treaties with the Cherokee Nation. If dealing with the Cherokee Nation was a federal issue, then from Worcester's point of view, the States had no authority to pass laws regarding those lands. Those State laws, according to Worcester, were unconstitutional and void, and were repugnant to the 1802 act of Congress entitled "An Act to regulate trade and intercourse with the Indian tribes." The superior court overruled the plea, and the plaintiff in error was tried, convicted, and sentenced to four years of hard labor.[53]

President Andrew Jackson entered the situation,

at this point, and the federal government proceeded to cite and admonish the State of Georgia for its actions. The State was commanded to appear before the United States Supreme Court, pursuant to a writ of error. Chief Justice Marshall delivered the opinion of the Court.[54]

Marshall's observation was that there were two questions at issue. First, are the treaties made by the United States with the Cherokee Nation valid? Second, was statute of the State of Georgia entitled "An Act to prevent the exercise of assumed and arbitrary power by all persons, under pretext of authority from the Cherokee Indians" valid? The act in question stated that all white people residing within the Cherokee Nation must conform to the rules of Georgia. These rules included obtaining a license or permit from a State official of Georgia allowing that person to live in the Cherokee Nation. The person would also have to take an oath to the State of Georgia, and, if the person failed to do so, they could be sentenced to a minimum of four years hard labor. Marshall wrote that the very passage of the act was an assertion of jurisdiction over the Cherokee Nation, and contrary to federal authority.[55]

John Marshall pointed out that Treaties between the United States and the Cherokee Nation goes back to before the founding of the country, based on the existence of previous treaties between the Indians and Great Britain. The United States, once the union became its own sovereign country, decided to receive the Cherokee Nation into their favor and protection. The U.S. Constitution refers to Indians not taxed in Article I, Section 2, Clause 3; and Article I, Section 8 of the Constitution states that "Congress shall have the power to regulate Commerce with foreign nations and among the several states, and *with the Indian tribes"*, therefore he recognized that while the Indian tribes were separate from the federal government, the states, and foreign nations, The Cherokee acknowledged themselves to be under the protection of the United States and no other power.[56]

Marshall reasoned that the only inference to be drawn from all of the evidence was that the United States considered the Cherokees as being a nation. Marshall wrote that multiple treaties between the United States and the Cherokee Nation existed, affirming the Cherokee Nation's right to self-government and its status as a distinct community. He explained that the Cherokees occupied their own territory as a sovereign and separate nation, therefore, the State of Georgia had no right to make legislation regarding those lands.

In conclusion, Marshall wrote that the act of the State of Georgia under which the plaintiff was prosecuted was void, and the forcible seizure and abduction of Worcester, who was residing in the Cherokee nation, with its permission, was a violation.[57]

Marshall's opinion established that the Indian Nations were all separate from the United States and exempt from the laws of the States of the Union that may surround their territory.[58]

President Jackson did not enforce the ruling, nor did the courts call the federal marshal to remove Worcester from the lands. Nonetheless, Worcester was freed by Georgia. Georgia complied after several months. The following year, in 1833, the newly elected governor, Wilson Lumpkin, offered to pardon Worcester and another individual named Butler if they ceased their activities among the Cherokee. The two complied and never returned to Cherokee land again.[59]

Interestingly enough, years later (1836-1839) the Trail of Tears commenced. President Jackson removed the Cherokees from their land to the "Indian Territory," known today as the State of Oklahoma. Jackson deemed that if the Cherokee Nation was to be under the protection of the federal government, as ruled by John Marshall, then a part of that protection must be to relocate them in order to appease the land and gold speculators in Georgia. After all, Marshall had not established protection *from* the federal government for the Indian Nations – only that the national government, not State governments, had authority over Indian affairs.[60]

While John Marshall was the primary force in early America rewriting the Constitution through case law so as to strengthen federal supremacy over the States, like a broken clock, he was not immune to occasionally coming to the correct conclusion. In *Barron v. Baltimore*, 1833, the Court held that the Bill of Rights was intended to apply only to the federal government, and therefore does not apply against the States.[61] The federal court system, however, after The War Between the States, has since largely incorporated the Bill of Rights with respect to the States, using the 14th Amendment as their excuse,[62] despite the fact that Congress overruled John Bingham's (writer of the equal protection and due process clauses of the 14th Amendment) desire to do so through the amendment and legislatively.[63]

• 3: Andrew Jackson

 The seventh president of the United States, Andrew Jackson is known as the Father of the Democratic Party. In most history books his fellow members of the party prior to Jackson's election are listed as "Democratic-Republican" (a term not used by the Jeffersonians – they called themselves "Republicans"), but Jackson is always listed as "Democrat."

Jackson was a war hero. When the people in Tennessee raised an army to fight the Creek Indians in 1802, Jackson was elected a major general in the Tennessee militia. While he had no military training, he proved to be an excellent general.[1] In the War of 1812, he led the Tennessee militia to victories over the Creek Indians (1813) and a large British force at the Battle of New Orleans (1815).[2] In 1817 Jackson led U.S. forces in the First Seminole War (1817-1818) and exceeding instructions, went on to invade Spanish West Florida.[3]

Though a soldier, Jackson, like many of his brethren in politics, was also a lawyer, and a well-respected one, at that. In 1787, at the age of twenty, after an apprenticeship...with an itinerant court and the tutelage of the convivial Colonel John Stokes...[Jackson] was declared by the court to be 'a person of unblemished moral character, and...competent...knowledge of the law.'"[4]

After the U.S. acquired Florida by treaty in 1821, he served as its first Territorial Governor. In 1796 Jackson served as Tennessee's first U.S. Representative (1796-97), was a U.S. Senator (1797-1798), and Judge of the State Superior Court (1798-1804).[5] He was elected again to the U.S. Senate in 1823. In 1824 he lost a bid for the presidency, but returned to achieve victory against the incumbent, John Quincy Adams, in 1828,[6] and two other candidates from his own party. The Whig Party did not form until 1833, and the Federalist Party had finally snorted its final whimper shortly after the previous presidential election (1824).

The United States was changing during Jackson's approach to the presidency. The northeast and the southern States had been the primary voices until Jackson reached the White House. "Old Hickory" found his pride in the frontier. He was born and raised in Tennessee, where the necessity of the lands to the west were more democratic, than based on the republican checks and balances of the Constitution.[7] While he appreciated the U.S. Constitution, and said that he believed in its principles, he believed that the "consent of the governed" and the will of "We the People" would be best served if the United States was a pure democracy.

Andrew Jackson was a firm believer in good economics, and ran on eliminating all of the United States' debt. He also ran his campaign on the idea of sending the Bank of the United States, a centralized system much like today's Federal Reserve, out of its charter.

The panic of 1819 had demonstrated what happened when money vanished; the next panic would spread more rapidly along the improved avenues of commerce.[8] Having been a merchant, Jackson recognized that the Bank of the United States was not fortunate in its choice of directors who first inflated the currency and then contracted it.[9]

The election of 1832 was a crucial one to the Bank, because the charter was to be renewed during the term of the president elected that year. Jackson promised the American people, "The Federal Constitution must be obeyed, state rights preserved, our national debt must be paid, direct taxes and loans avoided, and the Federal Union preserved."[10]

The re-chartering bill passed through Congress, "passed the Senate by a vote of 28 to 20 and the House by a vote by a vote of 107 to 85. But, President Jackson had the last opportunity to act on the Bill, so he vetoed it on July 10, 1832. In his veto, Jackson again warned the American people by saying, "It is regretted the rich and powerful too often bend the acts of governments to their selfish purposes. Distinctions in society will always exist under just government."[11]

In his speech, while technically accurate about the dangers to the American System when mercantilism (crony capitalism) is being engaged, in his words you can hear the root of the current feelings spouted by the modern day Democrat Party, and language in the 14th amendment which would be written and ratified after the War Between the States, and after the assassination of Abraham Lincoln.

Jackson continued, "Equality of talents, of education, of wealth, cannot be produced by human institutions. In the full enjoyment of the gifts of heaven, and the fruits of superior industry, economy and virtue, every man is equally entitled to protection by law, but when the law undertakes to these natural and just advantages artificial distinctions, to grant titles, gratuities and exclusive privileges, to make the rich richer, and the potent more powerful, the humble members of society – the farmers, mechanics, and laborers – who have neither the time nor the means of securing like favors to themselves, have a right to complain of their injustice to their government."[12]

In his veto message he explained that he wished to reorganize the bank into constitutionality. Jackson wrote, "A bank of the United States is in many respects convenient for the Government and useful to the people. Entertaining this opinion, and deeply impressed with the belief of some of the powers and privileges possessed by the existing bank are unauthorized by the Constitution, subversive of the rights of the States, and dangerous to the liberties of the people, I felt it my duty at an early period of my Administration to call the attention of Congress to the practicability of organizing an institution combining all its advantages and obviating these objections. I sincerely regret that in the act before me I can perceive none of those modification of the bank charter which are necessary, in my opinion, to make it compatible with justice, with sound policy, or with the Constitution of our country."[13]

Andrew Jackson viewed the Constitution as being a "People's Constitution." Jackson believed that in a republic there were too many remnants of the old European aristocracy, and he believed that not only was democracy the only true road to freedom, but that the existing political elite "stood ready to strike down any movement or activity that bore the slightest 'appearance of democracy.' Over and over in his letters he reiterated the inevitability and absolute justice of majority rule."[14]

After killing the Bank of the United States, Jackson launched his revolution for democracy. He had already been an integral part in reshaping the Electoral College.

"The process was never intended to be democratic…Not until [the] 1820s, with the rise of Andrew Jackson, did popular voting have a role in the selection of presidents…the Founders went to great lengths to insulate the activities of their new government from democratic pressures. One of the ways that they tried to limit their government from democracy was by selecting the nation's chief executive through the use of an electoral college, rather than through direct democratic election…by 1828, when Andrew Jackson was elected as president, the method of electing the president had almost completely transformed into the democratic system that still exists…This metamorphosis of the electoral college mirrors changes that have occurred more generally in American government during its first two centuries…Not only did the Founders not intend for public policy to be determined democratically, they actively tried to design their new government to prevent public policy from being directed by the demands of its citizens. They recognized that liberty could be compromised by democracy, and that the will of the majority had the potential to be just as tyrannical as a king or dictator…The electoral college was an important part of their attempt to limit the influence of democracy on American government…It is apparent from the wording of…the Constitution that the Founders did not intend for electors to be democratically elected…they did not intend the method of choice to dictate how the electors would cast their ballots…The Constitution has never bound electors to vote for specific candidates, and the Constitution makes it clear that the Founders envisioned electors using their discretion to select the candidates they viewed as best-qualified."[15]

Presidential elections were increasingly being decided by popular vote, with the big transition occurring in the 1820s. In the election of 1820, nine States still chose their electors in their State legislatures, but by 1824, when John Quincy Adams was elected, only six did. In 1828, when Andrew Jackson unseated Adams to become president, only two States had their legislatures choose their electors.[16]

The appointment of presidential electors by the legislature of the newly admitted State of Colorado in 1876 was the last occasion when presidential electors were not chosen by a direct vote of the people.[17]

Since 1832 the electors have voted 99% with the voting public. Also, in 1832, the winner-take-all rule became predominant throughout the country.[18]

The Founders tried to insulate the federal government from democratic control for what they believed were good reasons, and had no notion that the president would be chosen by the popular vote of American citizens. Yet the Democratic Party formed under Andrew Jackson, and through the efforts of Van Buren, for exactly that reason. Moving towards democracy was an unqualified success for the Democrats. Jackson won the presidency in 1828, defeating the incumbent president by an electoral total of 178 to 83. After Jackson's two terms as president, Van Buren was elected president for one term, and was unseated by his Whig challenger William Henry Harrison in 1840.[19]

Andrew Jackson claimed he wished to reduce the scope and power of the federal government, and indeed his policies did just that. He believed democracy to be a means by the people to control the federal government, but, he may not have realized that in truth democracy is a transitional government that historically has always given way to tyranny through oligarchy – something the Founding Fathers, who appreciated Thomas Jefferson's allegiance to *laissez faire,* fully understood.

Karl Marx (1818-1883), who was a student of German philosopher Georg Wilhelm Friedrich Hegel (1770-1831), was formulating his theories about communism at about the same time. In his writings, Marx expressed the belief that the working class could achieve power through democratic elections, and that the working class had the right to revolt if they were denied political expression through democratic means. As a result, the quote "Democracy is the road to socialism" is often attributed to him.[20]

Oblivious, or perhaps not, to the fact that pure

democracy was going to become the weapon of choice by those who sought to expand the scope and power of the federal government in the near future, Jackson believed and promoted that the top officials in the government should only be elected directly, including Senators (which came to pass in 1913 with the ratification of the 17th Amendment). Then, once elected, the democratically elected officials should heed the wishes of the electorate, knowing that if they did not, popular election would give voters a direct method of also removing from office officials who did not further the will of the people. Jackson argued that popular elections create an incentive structure that holds elected officials more accountable to the demands of the voters. He believed that through democracy the federal government could be wrested from the control of the political elite who had allegedly been overseeing it since the ratification of the Constitution.

Jackson had not been educated in the same manner as his predecessors, so his philosophies regarding democracy were a knee-jerk reaction to his perception of what the system had been. He believed that the republican experiment was failing, and that it had been accumulating power in the hands of a relentless political elite. Democracy was the mechanism he believed could redistribute the power away from the elite, and return it to the people.

Jackson argued that he was saving the Constitution, when in reality democracy would ultimately place the Constitution in jeopardy. Rather than adhere to the Constitution, pure democracy encourages politicians to worry more about making the electorate happy, so they begin to pander to popular opinion, and provide gifts from the treasury in the form of subsidies and benefits.

Jackson's play for democracy was nothing new. Alexander Hamilton, and his allies, understood that democracy was the way to expand the scope and power of the federal government. Five times James Madison wrote in his Federalist Essays the difference between a republic and a democracy.[21] At the time, for the purpose of pushing democracy, and compromising the U.S. Constitution, the followers of Hamilton's philosophies of nationalism were proclaiming that there is no difference between a republic and a democracy. While Jackson was successful, so was Hamilton, albeit a little more than three decades after his death at the hands of Aaron Burr's dueling pistol.

Hamilton got the ball rolling, and Jackson launched it into full gear, creating a lasting legacy that has progressed over two centuries – making the federal government more democratic, and thus more oriented toward satisfying the demands of the voters rather than protecting their liberty.[22]

In the Founder's version of America as a republic, they believed there must be multiple constituencies. Therefore, the voice of the States needed to be as important, and loud, as the voice of the people. They believed their version of the Electoral College would curb the rise of mass democracy and the loss of liberty it invites. The failure of the States to stand up for themselves, and their rights, as a part of the constituency – and the obvious appeal or pure democracy (amidst the cry of "the will of the people") – has led us to a moment in history where it is commonly accepted that the United States is a democracy. Beginning with Alexander Hamilton and Andrew Jackson, the United States has been incrementally, and fundamentally, changed into something the Founding Fathers never intended.

• 4: Joseph Story

Born during the Revolutionary War, Joseph Story became the protégé of John Marshall. Like Marshall, Story claimed to be a defender of the United States Constitution. He served on the Supreme Court of the United Sates from 1811 to 1845, never achieving the position of Chief Justice.

In 1833, Story published his "Commentaries on the Constitution of the United States." The work has become a cornerstone of judicial interpretation of the Constitution, and a large part in the creation of today's web of case law through judicial review.

While Story opposed Jacksonian democracy,[1] he was a follower of the philosophies of Alexander Hamilton and John Marshall. After Marshall's death, Story continued to carry the torch, shaping American Law in Hamilton's image.[2]

Joseph Story was the son of Dr. Elisha Story, a member of the Sons of Liberty who took part in the

Boston Tea Party. He graduated from Harvard in 1798. At the time he was aligned with the Jeffersonian Republicans.[3]

He served in the Massachusetts House of Representatives from 1805 to 1808. Story became a member of the United States House of Representatives in 1808, where he served until March of 1809. He returned to the Massachusetts House of Representatives after that, becoming the Speaker of the State House in 1811.[4]

November 1811, at the age of thirty-two, Joseph Story became the youngest member of the United States Supreme Court. He was nominated by President James Madison, and was sworn in and assumed office on February 3, 1812.[5]

As his time on the court proceeded, Story became one of Chief Justice John Marshall's most trusted allies, and according to historian Clinton Rossiter, "the most Hamiltonian of judges."[6]

Story carried on the belief that the States were not the creators of the federal government, but that it was a creation of the "whole people".[7]

A nationalist, Story's judicial opinions became more and more Marshall-like as time passed. Early on, with the *Martin v. Hunter's Lessee* (1816) opinion, one that Marshall decided to take no part in the consideration or decision of, Story established himself as a champion for the rise of federal supremacy. Joseph Story argued that the power to interpret a treaty was not granted by the States, but by the people democratically. Therefore, the Supremacy Clause applies, allowing the "federal" Supreme Court's interpretation to trump the State's interpretation in any case involving treaties. Ultimately, the case established that the United States Supreme Court has the authority over State courts in all civil matters of federal law.[8]

Story's decision in the *Fairfax's Devisee v. Hunter Lessee* (1813) case fueled already intense criticism of the Court. States' rights advocates claimed Story had reduced the States to mere administrative units lacking real sovereignty. The Virginia judiciary refused to enter the judgment, effectively denying the validity of the claim that the federal courts were supreme over the State courts. The Virginia judges stated that they were under no obligation to obey the Supreme Court.[9]

Virginia's refusal to comply led to the *Martin v. Hunter's Lessee* case. As with the previous case, John Marshall recused himself, so Story grabbed the reins, and again wrote the opinion.

Story rebuked Virginia for failing to comply with the Court's previous order. He also rejected Virginia's claim that it was equally sovereign with the United States. "We the People" at the beginning of the Preamble, argued Story, reveals that the American people created the nation and lodged the national judicial power exclusively in the federal court system. He also channeled Alexander Hamilton, insisting that the government possesses certain implied powers, and that the power to interpret the Constitution had to rest with one ultimate source of authority, which was the United States Supreme Court.[10]

John Marshall doubled down on Story's argument three years later in upholding the Bank of the United States in *McCulloch v. Maryland* (1819).[11]

Joseph Story also received a great deal of fame regarding his participation in the Amistad case, which energized a fledgling abolitionist movement and finally forced slavery into a position of intensified political conflict.

While, throughout his career as a Supreme Court Justice, Story did what he could to uphold federal judicial supremacy over the States, the Amistad case created a controversy that was a key component in eventually silencing States' Rights for good.

The period was marked as being a time of massacres, largely carried out in the wake of *Turner's Revolt* so as to terrorize black communities. Amistad was one of two mutinies on two slave-trading ships, which were operating at a time after the United States Congress had passed legislation disallowing any States in the union to participate in the Atlantic slave trade.[12]

The 1839 mutiny aboard the *Amistad* was led by Joseph Cinqué, son of an African king, who led fifty-four Africans being transported to the New World in a revolt that attempted to steer the vessel back to their homeland. Instead, the ship was guided by some of the ship's crewmen toward the Connecticut coast[13] where the Africans were interned until the United States Supreme Court, with Joseph Story taking the lead, freed them.

When the *Amistad* began to drift towards the American Coast, two sea captains, Peletiah Fordham and Henry Green, saw the boat approaching. When they were close enough to communicate with the people they could see on the boat, they realized the people were black, and likely slaves being transported into the New World. They assured the blacks who seemed to be in control of the vessel that they were not in slave-holding country. The blacks told Fordham and Green that there were two trunks full of gold aboard the schooner, and that they would be given to whoever outfitted them with provisions and helped them sail back to their African homeland. Green suggested that if they got the trunks he would help them return to Africa.[14]

Before Green and Fordham could cash in, a brig of the U. S. Coast Guard, the *Washington*, interfered. The commander of the brig, Lieutenant Thomas Gedney, boarded the schooner and ordered, at gunpoint, all hands below the deck. Two Spaniards emerged from below, telling the American commander a tale of mutiny, blood, deceit, and desperation aboard the *Amistad*.[15]

The slaves on board were recently brought from Africa and brought to Cuba in direct contravention of an 1817 treaty between Spain and Britain prohibiting the importation of slaves to Spanish colonies. They had been eluding British ships that patrolled the waters, and had purposely steered clear of United States waters because the American Congress had outlawed participation in the Atlantic Slave Trade by The States in 1808.[16]

The *Amistad* was towed to New London, Connecticut. The United States Attorney for Connecticut, William S. Holabird, ordered a judicial hearing, more interested in salvage rights, than whether or not there was a crime committed. The *Amistad's* cargo of wine, saddles, gold, and silk was worth an estimated $40,000 in 1839 dollars, and the slaves had a market value of at least half that much.[17]

The district judge for Connecticut, Andrew T. Judson, who was an appointee of President Andrew Jackson, at the end of the hearing, made a motion with his hand to his throat to suggest a hanging. He wound up referring the case, however, for trial in Circuit Court, where in 1839 all federal criminal trials were held. The Africans were put into custody at the county jail in New Haven.[18]

For New England's abolitionists, the case surrounding the *Amistad* presented an opportunity. The "Amistad Committee" was quickly formed for the purpose of helping the Africans, ultimately enlisting the legal help of Roger Baldwin, who would later become the governor of Connecticut.[19]

Spain was demanding a return of the schooner *Amistad* and its passengers to its Cuban owners, stating that U.S. courts had no jurisdiction over Spanish subjects. While the Van Buren Administration was anxious to comply with the Spanish demands, constitutionalists of the period demanded that the matter still be put through a due process of law.[20]

The Circuit Court heard the case on September 14, 1839. The *Amistad* slaves and crew were sent to Hartford for their trial in the Circuit courtroom of Judge Smith Thompson, who also served as a justice on the United States Supreme Court. Baldwin argued that "no power on earth has the right to reduce [the Africans] to slavery" and the United States should never stoop so low as to become a "slave-catcher for foreign slave-holders." Judge Thompson wanted to avoid it becoming a political debate over abolition, resting his decision on jurisdictional grounds. He decided after three days of argument that because the alleged mutiny and murders occurred in international waters and did not involve U.S. citizens, the court had no jurisdiction to consider the criminal charges.[21]

As for the question about whether or not the slaves could be considered as "property" of who claimed to be their slaveholders, Judge Thompson ruled that was a matter to be decided by the district court. Thompson ruled that the Africans, although no longer considered prisoners, should be detained until the district court could decide whether they were property and--if they were property--who owned them.[22]

It was eventually determined the Africans were originally from a region south of Freetown in what is now Sierra Leone. A speaker of their language, James Covey, was brought to New Haven, and it was then that the full story of the Africans' adventures began to come out. The *Amistad* captives had first met at a slave factory after having been kidnapped by African slavers. Along with about 600 other Africans, they were loaded aboard the Portuguese ship *Tecora* and taken via the infamous "Middle Passage" across the Atlantic. The slaves were kept naked, flogged for not eating, and chained in a half-lying position. Many died at sea and were tossed overboard. Landing at night in Havana, they were taken to the slave market where ten days later they were bought by the Spaniards in charge of the *Amistad*.[23]

During the voyage, The African Prince, Cinqué, used a nail to break the chain that fastened all the slaves to the wall, and the mutiny began.[24]

The time in America, during the legal trials, brought its own trials. The harsh weather was new to the Africans, as was the food, the diseases, and the reality that a return home may not be happening anytime soon.[25]

The civil trial regarding the *Amistad* began on November 19, 1839 in Hartford. After two days of testimony, the trial was adjourned until January 7, 1840. In the New Haven harbor was the naval schooner *Grampus*, sent there by President Van Buren to sail the Africans of the *Amistad* back to Cuba should the court rule, as expected, in the government's favor. Van Buren's secret orders provided that the Africans were to be rushed immediately to the ship and placed in irons before an appeal could be filed, and that the *Grampus* should sail for Havana unless an "appeal shall actually have been interposed."[26]

According to Baldwin and his team, the Africans were illegally imported from Africa and were therefore the property of no one. Dr. Josiah Gibbs Sr., a linguistics expert, testified that the Africans spoke Mende, not Spanish, proving their place of origin.[27] The story of their capture and subsequent adventures by the Africans left the Americans in the courtroom listening "with breathless attention." The New Haven Herald reported that he "manifested a high degree of sagacity, of keenness, and decision."[28] Sullivan Haley testified that Ruiz, one of the Spaniards who had purchased the Africans in

Havana, before being sent back to Cuba, had admitted that the captives were not legal slaves. Dr. Richard Madden, an abolitionist and the British anti-slavery commissioner in Cuba, stated the Cuban slave market where the Africans had been bought had been raided only months earlier by British authorities. He described how Cuban authorities "winked at the slave trade in return for $10 to $15 a slave," using fraudulent documents to deceive inspectors, and would without hesitation kill the *Amistad* blacks should they be returned to Cuba.[29]

The Spanish consul claimed the *Amistad* blacks be returned to Spain.[30]

Judge Judson announced his decision on January 13, 1840, after a weekend of deliberation. He ruled that the *Amistad* captives were "born free" and kidnapped in violation of international law. They had mutinied, he said, out of a "desire of winning their liberty and of returning to their families and kindred." He ordered that the Amistad Africans be "delivered to President Van Buren for transport back to Africa."[31]

However, the *Grampus* sailed out of New Haven harbor without its black passengers. Van Buren was described as "greatly dissatisfied."[32]

The Van Buren Administration appealed the district court's decision, sending the case to the United States Supreme Court. The makeup of the Supreme Court at the time consisted of five southerners who either owned or had owned slaves, out of the total of nine justices.[33]

John Quincy Adams was asked to argue the Africans' case before the Supreme Court of the United States in Washington. Former President Adams, then 74 and a member of Congress, at first resisted, pleading age and infirmity. But, Adams believed firmly in the rightness of the cause, and eventually agreed to join Baldwin in arguments before the Court. "By the blessing of God, I will argue the case before the Supreme Court," Adams was quoted as saying. He wrote in his diary: "I implore the mercy of God to control my temper, to enlighten my soul, and to give me utterance, that I may prove myself in every respect equal to the task."[34]

A month later, Adams shook hands with Cinqué and his African countrymen, telling them "God willing, we will make you free."[35]

On Monday, February 22, 1841, arguments began in the Supreme Court's crowded chamber in the U.S. Capitol. Francis Scott Key, author of the "Star Spangled Banner" and now an attorney, was present, and offered his advice to Adams on the case. Attorney General Henry Gilpin, arguing for the government, told the Court that it should not "go behind" the *Amistad's* papers and make inquiry as to their accuracy, but should accept them on their face in order to show proper respect for another sovereign nation.   Roger Baldwin followed Gilpin, making many of the same arguments that been persuasive in the district and circuit courts.[36]

John Quincy Adams began his argument on February 24th, stating that if the President had the power to send the Africans to Cuba, he would equally as well have the power to seize forty Americans and send them overseas for trial. He argued that Spain was asking the President to "first turn man-robber...next turn jailer...and lastly turn catchpole and convey them to Havana, to appease the vengeance of the African slave-traders of the barracoons."   He attacked the President for his ordering a naval vessel to stand ready in New Haven harbor, he attacked a southern intellectual's defense of slavery, and he quoted the Declaration of Independence: "The moment you come to the Declaration of Independence, that every man has a right to life and liberty, an inalienable right, this case is decided. I ask nothing more in behalf of these unfortunate men than this Declaration."[37]

Adams ended his Supreme Court argument on a personal, reflective note: "May it please your Honors: On the 7th of February, 1804, now more than thirty-seven years past, my name was entered, and yet stands recorded, on both the rolls, as one of the Attorneys and Counselors of this Court.   Five years later, in February and March, 1809, I appeared for the last time before this Court, in defense of the cause of justice, and of important rights, in which many of my fellow-citizens had property to a large amount at stake. Very shortly afterwards, I was called to the discharge of other duties--first in distant lands, and in later years, within our own country, but in different departments of her Government. Little did I imagine that I should ever again be required to claim the right of appearing in the capacity of an office of this Court; yet such has been the dictate of my destiny--and I appear again to plead the cause of justice and now of liberty and life, in behalf of many of my fellow men, before the same Court, which in a former age, I had addressed in support of rights of property. I stand again, I trust for the last time, before the same Court--hic caestus, artemque repono. I stand before the same Court, but not before the same judges--nor aided by the same associates--nor resisted by the same opponents. As I cast my eyes along those seats of honor and of public trust, now occupied you, they seek in vain for one of those honored and honorable persons whose indulgence listened then to my voice. Marshall--Cushing--Chase--Washington--Johnson--Livingston--Todd-- Where are they? . . . Where is the marshal--where are the criers of the Court? Alas! where is one of the very judges of the Court, arbiters of life and death, before whom I commenced this anxious argument, even now prematurely closed? Where are they all? Gone! Gone! All gone!-- Gone from the services which, in their day and generation, they faithfully rendered to their country. . . . In taking, then, my final leave of this Bar, and of this Honorable Court, I can only ejaculate a fervent petition to Heaven, that every member of it may go to his final account with as little of earthly frailty to answer for as those illustrious dead, and that you may, every one, after the close of a long and virtuous career in this world, be received at the portals of the next with the approving sentence, 'Well done, good and faithful servant; enter thou into the joy of thy Lord.'"[38]

Joseph Story spoke for the court on March 9, 1841 to announce the Supreme Court's decision. Justice Story said that the Amistads were "kidnapped Africans, who by the laws of Spain itself were entitled to their freedom." As justification for the Court's decision, Justice Story relied largely on the narrower arguments of Roger Baldwin, rather than the "interesting remarks" of John Quincy Adams.[39]

The Africans were free: they could stay or they could return to Africa. While not considered a repudiation of slavery, the decision clearly implied that if the Amistad Africans had been brought from Africa prior to the 1820 treaty banning importation of slaves, they would have been considered property of the Spaniards who had purchased them, Ruiz and Montes, and they would have been returned to Cuba.[40]

Adams wrote that he was filled with "great joy." Evangelical abolitionists saw an opportunity for the Amistads to become a key to an effort to bring Christianity to black Africa. The Spanish government was angered and somewhat mystified by the Court's action, subsequently beginning a long series of unsuccessful diplomatic efforts to obtain indemnification for loss of the *Amistad* and her cargo.[41]

After various efforts to raise the money necessary to transport the Amistads back to their Mende homeland, accompanied by problematic events including a suicide, an assault, racial taunts, and in the case of Cinqué a brawl with some local rowdies, the time to leave finally arrived. November, 1841, the ship *Gentleman* was chartered for $1,840 to carry the Africans back to Freetown, where the Governor of Sierra Leone said the group would be met and guided on a four-day journey to Mendeland. After a moving and tearful round of goodbyes, the thirty-five surviving Africans of the *Amistad*, and four American missionaries, boarded the *Gentleman* and departed for West Africa.[42]

After fifty days at sea, the *Gentleman* put down anchor in Freetown harbor. After the arrival, the Africans resorted by to their "heathenish dancing." British missionaries in Freetown told the Americans that their plan to establish a mission in Mendeland was folly. The American missionaries wrote letters home complaining of their *Amistad* students, that they had fallen back into their "licentious habits." Rats, malaria, and yellow fever also haunted the endeavors of the missionaries. One by one, the missionaries died and were replaced by others. The last of the *Amistad* Africans to have contact with the mission was Cinqué. In 1879, old and emaciated, he stumbled into the mission to die and was buried among the graves of the American missionaries.[43]

Spain was never compensated for the loss of the Amistad, either. John Quincy Adams led the opposition to compensation efforts until his death in 1847, calling the proposal "a robbery of the people of the United States." With the election of Abraham Lincoln in 1860, Spain's efforts came to an end.[44]

Joseph Story's career came to an end with his death. He died while still holding a position as an Associate Justice of the Supreme Court of the United States at the age of 65, on September 10, 1845. His primary legacy was a three volume work titled "Commentaries on the Constitution of the United States" published in 1833. His commentaries have served as an important part of case law, fueling the judicial system's Hamiltonian interpretation of Constitutional Law.[45] The written commentaries by Story, even today, continues to be revered by legal professionals who support the concepts of judicial review and case law as being the "rule of law." Unfortunately, while some of the entries by Story are in line with original intent, a significant portion of his writings defend John Marshall's viewpoint of the U.S. Constitution, and have been an integral part of the journey of the court system from being the weakest branch of government to becoming a judicial oligarchy.

The legacy of Joseph Story, like that of John Marshall, lives on, and continues to serve as a tool used by those who wish to dismantle the U.S. Constitution, and compromise the liberty established for this country by the Framers in 1787. Judicial activism owes much of its power to the writings and judicial opinions of Joseph Story, as the growing power of the judicial branch continues to advance the anti-American characteristics that are designed to ultimately establish a Hamiltonian America through the assistance of radical judicial betrayal of the U.S. Constitution and a growing culture of Marxism.

• 5: Franklin Delano Roosevelt

Franklin Delano Roosevelt became President of the United States during the Great Depression on March 4, 1933.[1] He was elected in November of 1932, and the atmosphere was a grim one. "The gaudy balloon of jazz age prosperity had split at the seams three years previously, plummeting the American people to the depths of privation and despair. Millions were out of work in the summer of 1932, and millions more worked or farmed for a pittance. In the Middle West, farmers receiving two cents a quart for milk resorted to a desperate measure to restore prices: they began dumping milk bound for the market…For millions of Americans, the only sign of hope on the horizon lay in the election of the Democratic candidate for President, Franklin D. Roosevelt, with his promise of a New Deal."[2]

Early, during the rise of FDR, he defended the U.S. Constitution, well knowing the importance of the document to the American people. Even during his presidency, as he was usurping the U.S. Constitution, President Roosevelt claimed to be its defender.

During his first inaugural address, March 4, 1933, Roosevelt said, "Our Constitution is so simple and practical that it is possible always to meet extraordinary needs by changes in emphasis and arrangement without loss of essential form."[3]

In a "Fireside Chat" on March 9, 1937, during which he used the words "constitution," "constitutional," and "unconstitutional" 41 times, President Roosevelt remarked, "I hope that you have re-read the Constitution of the United States in these past few weeks. Like the Bible, it ought to be read again and again."[4]

It was clear, however, years prior, that Roosevelt held a Hamiltonian view of the Constitution, defending the concept that it contains *implied powers*. During an address as Governor of New York, March 2, 1930, he said, "The United States Constitution has proved itself the most marvelously *elastic* compilation of rules of government ever written."[5] [emphasis added]

Roosevelt may have voiced his love for the U.S. Constitution, but contrary to our founding principles, he believed that soft socialism was what could pull the United States out of the economic difficulties she was in. His legislative strategies not only were socialist in nature, but were founded upon Marshall's concept of federal supremacy.

The 1932 Presidential Election represented a shift in America's political identity. While Roosevelt avoided specifics, he made clear that his program for economic recovery would make extensive use of the power of the federal government. He promised aid to farmers, public development of electric power, a balanced budget, and government policing of irresponsible private economic power. Roosevelt won the election in an electoral landslide, 472 to 59. Americans also elected substantial Democrat Party majorities to both Houses of Congress.[6]

Roosevelt had every tool he wanted for implementing his policies, except for the court system – an apparent frustration of his in 1937, when in his March 9 "Fireside Chat," he stated, "We must save the Constitution from the [Supreme] Court and the Court from itself."[7]

In 1937 President Franklin Roosevelt attempted to increase the number of justices to fifteen so that he could get a court which would be sympathetic to many of his New Deal programs. This was rejected, but a bill was passed which allowed the Attorney General to appeal directly to the Supreme Court whenever the constitutionality of an act of Congress was involved.[8]

In 1933, Roosevelt's Inauguration Address promised prompt, decisive action, and he conveyed some of his own unshakable self-confidence to millions of Americans listening on radios throughout the land. "This great nation will endure as it has endured, will revive and prosper," he asserted, adding, "the only thing we have to fear is fear itself."[9]

Act One of the coming New Deal nightmare breached its legislative birth canal in 1933 with the delivery of the National Industrial Recovery Act, which was believed to represent the kind of reform the nation needed. [Roosevelt's wife,] Eleanor, hoped the NRA [National Recovery Act] codes would be charters of "fair play" among the various elements in the industrial process...she helped the unions in their drive to organize...and when the codes turned into agreements for administered prices and restricted production she did her utmost to get consumer representation on the code authorities and state recovery boards.[10]

The next program in 1933 was the Agricultural Adjustment Act. It seemed senseless when people were starving and in rags to pay farmers to plow under cotton and slaughter piglets, which had been a practice in an effort to influence farm prices. In reference to the piglets, she once told a farmer, "There are thousands of people in the country starving. Why not give the meat away to them?"

Her position led to a scheme that anticipated the food-stamp plan.[11]

While on the surface the plans of President Roosevelt, and Eleanor's opinions of them, seemed to be a good thing, increasing federal authority over the interior issues of the United States was contrary to Jefferson's championed concept of *laissez faire*. The policies of the Roosevelt administration seemed utopian and socialist, because they were.

During the autumn of 1933, Eleanor Roosevelt became a fan of the book, *Prohibiting Poverty*, by Prestonia Mann Martin, the granddaughter of Horace Mann.[12] Horace Mann was an early reformer of education, as well as a member of the United States House of Representatives from 1848 to 1853.[13]

The Mann family went on to find itself among the ranks of Fabians here in the States.[14]

Prestonia Mann was a contributing editor of *The American Fabian*.[15] In an April 6th, 1945 obit in the Winter Park Topics, the following was pointed out: "Under the name of Prestonia Mann Martin she gained international fame from her sociological thesis, 'Prohibiting Poverty,' which proposed a remedy for periodical depressions by a division of labor and a distribution of the necessities of life under government regulation. Her proposal brought comment and a large measure of approval from leaders of thought all over the world. Mrs. Eleanor

Roosevelt gave the book favorable comment in her public statements."[16]

Like his wife Eleanor, President Roosevelt supported socialism, and supported the Democrat Party's claim that the United States is a democracy, likely well knowing that as a democracy it would be easier to steer the United States towards socialism. In a speech on January 6, 1941, he spoke of the United States as the "arsenal of democracy," and declared that American policy in the world crisis was governed by the search for "four essential human freedoms: freedom of speech and expression throughout the world, freedom of worship, freedom from want and freedom from fear."[17]

During the speech he specifically remarked that "every realist knows that the democratic way of life is at this moment being directly assailed in every part of the world."[18]

In a Campaign Address at Cleveland, Ohio on November 2, 1940, Roosevelt said, "You and I are proud of that opposition. It is positive proof that what we have built and strengthened in the past seven years is democracy...We Americans of today—all of us—we are characters in this living book of democracy."[19]

In a "Message for American Education Week", September 27, 1938, President Roosevelt said, "Democracy cannot succeed unless those who express their choice are prepared to choose wisely. The real safeguard of democracy, therefore, is education. It has been well said that no system of government gives so much to the individual or exacts so much as a democracy. Upon our educational system must largely depend the perpetuity of those institutions upon which our freedom and our security rest. To prepare each citizen to choose wisely and to enable him to choose freely are paramount functions of the schools in a democracy."[20]

Like his counterpart, Adolf Hitler, Roosevelt understood the importance of training the younger generation in the ideology you wish the next generation to follow. While his long list of New Deal programs did not technically directly influence the education system in the country,[21] the New Deal programs did have a significant effect on education in the United States.

America's schools were in need of help, so Roosevelt's federal government came to the rescue, providing immediate relief in the form of a $20 million federal appropriation that was used to help shore up schools and districts most in danger of collapse. While the move was welcomed by the educational establishment in the country, the National Educational Association (NEA) hoped FDR's action would remain in keeping with the traditional view of the federal government's relationship to education: providing funds to support

State and local districts, but not getting involved in policy. Encouraged by the President's initial move, the NEA held out the hope that such aid would continue, which was a big change from the policies of past administrations. Direct federal support for State and local schools prior to 1933 was not common, nor encouraged. The New Deal spent massive numbers of dollars to support education, but most of these funds did not take the form of direct support for State and local districts. Nor were they spent or even overseen by the recently-created Department of Education, which opened in 1931. Rather, most of the money spent came under the auspices of such New Deal agencies as the Works Progress Administration, the National Youth Administration, and even the Civilian Conservation Corps.[22]

While some may have championed the new interest in education by the federal government, largely because of the reports of a widespread epidemic of illiteracy, the truth was that the century and a half constitutionally grounded concept of education only residing in the hands of the local communities was not only being challenged, but washed away. While The Office of Education had been created by Abraham Lincoln's Republicans in 1867,[23] its role didn't increase until Roosevelt's administration got a hold of it. Eventually, the department was done away with in 1972, only to be resurrected again in 1979 by the Jimmy Carter administration.[24] Carter's Department of Education, however, took Roosevelt's intrusion into the institution to a whole new level, creating a leviathan that I tend to refer to as the "Department of Indoctrination".

By the time the Roosevelt administration was nothing more than a footnote in history, it was realized that Roosevelt's policies prolonged the length of the depression in the United States; an unfortunate turn that the liberal left, even to this day, denies. In reality, shortening the economic catastrophe was not really the plan, anyway. For the most ardent observer, it is easy to believe that the real plan, all along, had been to strengthen the power of the federal government, while usurping the limiting principles contained on the pages of the United States Constitution.

Author John T. Flynn argues that history gives Roosevelt too much credit for knowing what he was doing. He argues that, "Fundamentally he was without any definite political or economic philosophy. He was not a man to deal in fundamentals. . . . The positions he took on political and economic questions were not taken in accordance with deeply rooted political beliefs but under the influence of political necessity. . . . He was in every sense purely an opportunist."[25]

Despite the denials that Roosevelt was a socialist, in today's political environment, it is the anti-constitution socialists who revere FDR the most.

In 2015, self-proclaimed socialist, Bernie Sanders, "sought to wrap himself in the mantle of Franklin D. Roosevelt...[comparing] his brand of democratic socialism with references to the successful efforts by the New Deal architect — who has also featured in Hillary Clinton's campaign...[Sanders said,] 'Against the ferocious opposition of the ruling class of his day, people he called economic royalists, Roosevelt implemented a series of programs that put millions of people back to work, took them out of poverty, and restored our faith in government. He redefined the relationship of the federal government to the people of our nation. He combated cynicism, fear and despair. He reinvigorated democracy. He transformed the country, and that is what we have to do today...And, by the way, almost everything he proposed, almost every program, every idea, was called socialist.' Sanders' address...stuck primarily to domestic policy — referring frequently to Roosevelt, Martin Luther King, Jr., and Pope Francis...'Let me define for you, simply and straightforwardly, what democratic socialism means to me. It builds on what Franklin Delano Roosevelt said when he fought for guaranteed economic rights for all Americans,' Sanders explained. 'And it builds on what Martin Luther King, Jr. said in 1968, when he stated that, 'this country has socialism for the rich and rugged individualism for the poor.' It builds on the success of many other countries around the world who have done a far better job than we have in protecting the needs of their working families, their elderly citizens, their children, their sick and their poor...It's time we had democratic socialism for working families, not just Wall Street, billionaires and large corporations. It means that we should not be providing welfare for corporations, huge tax breaks for the very rich, or trade policies which would boost corporate profits as workers lose their job.'"[26]

The legacy of Franklin Delano Roosevelt has reinforced the belief that federal government programs offer the only remedy for economic downturns and poverty. In 2008, presidential candidate Hillary Clinton proclaimed she would appoint a new "secretary of poverty" whose position would be tasked with "ending poverty as we know it in America."[27]

Americans, thanks to Roosevelt's New Deal legacy, which has been reported as being a great success by liberal-left-controlled academia and the news media, instinctively approve of the concept of the government providing programs to help society cope with the reality of poverty.

For today's Americans, the story is an old one. The Great Depression, we have been told, erupted after the unrestrained greed of fat cats and speculators led to the stock market crash in 1929, leaving defenseless average Americans suffering through hard times. The period included bank closures, stockholders leaping to their deaths from upper-story windows and off of bridges, and once stable laborers resorting to selling their belongings or fruit from their trees on street corners. Many of them, we are told, became vagrants and hobos, traveling on railcars from town to town, or living in shantytowns, looking for work, and finding none. Then, President Franklin Delano Roosevelt became President, and he saved the day, inspiring new hope with his flurry of radical reforms, and as a result he was rewarded with four terms as President.

My grandfather resorted to being a sharecropper, a type of farming in which families rent small plots of land from a landowner in return for a portion of their crop, to be given to the landowner at the end of each year. Grandma and Grandpa lived in a one room shack with no floor, so they lived on the dust. They had one cot, and an outhouse structure outside over a deep hole in the ground for their bodily waste. He entered World War II, shortly after. Grandma found work when all of the men went off to war, and retired as a grocery clerk many decades later. After returning from Europe, Grandpa tried a series of entrepreneurial ideas, finally landing on carpet installer. Not bad for an Irishman married to a girl from the Blackfoot tribe.

My grandparents never personally benefitted from Roosevelt's New Deal programs. But, nonetheless, they idolized Roosevelt, and a sure way to get Grandma to pick up her purse and walk out of the room without so much as a word would be to say something negative about Roosevelt, or any of his

Democrat Party successors.

As a result of the affectionate memories of Roosevelt from that generation, a false appreciation for federal intrusion into the matters of the States has emerged. It shapes political debate, and has served as a continuous nudge against the American System, steadily pushing it towards a utopianism the Founding Fathers never originally intended.

In 1993, during his First Inaugural Address, President Bill Clinton cited FDR's big government commitments, adding his own twist by saying, "We must provide for our nation the way a family provides for its children."[28]

Clinton viewed Americans as being helpless kids who can't support themselves, so the government "must provide."

Not a very far cry from Bernie Sanders' version of socialism we were able to get better acquainted with in the 2016 Presidential Election.

Both of them sounded to me like they were just handing us another version of Karl Marx's famous quote, "From each according to his ability, to each according to his needs."[29]

Roosevelt's legacy, overall, is that of higher tax burdens and a corresponding loss of liberty.

In reality, the end of the Great Depression finally arrived not because of Roosevelt's big government policies, but because the economic engine of the free market was finally able to grab hold of some growth after the end of World War II.

Historically, evidence reveals that the best remedy for ending recessions is to increase governmental restraint. Other major contractions and increased unemployment occurred in 1815, 1837, 1873, 1893, 1920, 1958, and 1979; and in each case the record consistently shows that leaders who cut government to revive the economy succeeded far more quickly and painlessly than did the New Deal.[30]

Despite the absence of federal programs (which was consistent with the Constitution's limited list of authorities to the federal government) the nineteenth century in America remained an unprecedented era of social and economic mobility. The Horatio Alger stories that became best sellers and inspired the nation reflected reality, as American families (including those of newly arrived immigrant masses) rose from abject poverty to middle-class status (or above) in one, two, or three generations. Social programs didn't power this escalator to prosperity; economic growth did.[31]

This is why the U.S. Constitution does not authorize the federal government to interfere with internal issues. When it does, the only thing accomplished is a rise of misery, and a few more steps along the journey towards tyranny, and bondage.

FDR, himself, understood what he was doing when he circumvented the U.S. Constitution. His speeches included "chilling language reminiscent of the fascist dictatorships simultaneously taking shape in Europe."[32]

"If we are to go forward," Roosevelt declared in his first Inauguration Speech, "we must move as a trained and loyal army willing to sacrifice for the good of a common discipline, because without such discipline no progress is made, no leadership becomes effective. We are, I know, ready and willing to submit our lives and property to such discipline. With this pledge taken, I assume unhesitatingly the leadership of this great army of our people dedicated to a disciplined attack on our common problems…it is to be hoped that the normal balance of executive and legislative authority may be wholly adequate to meet the unprecedented task before us. But it may be that an unprecedented demand and need for undelayed action may call for temporary departure from that normal balance of public procedure."[33]

In his very first speech as President of the United States Franklin Delano Roosevelt called for a suspension of constitutional rule; and the crowds cheered.[34]

DOUGLAS V. GIBBS

• 6: Lyndon B. Johnson

President Lyndon B. Johnson was more than merely a constitutional liar. He was a civil rights liar and a political power broker for socialism and the anti-Christian leftists.

It was Johnson, who, as a Senator in 1954, birthed the "Johnson Amendment." The legislative victory for Johnson, designed to undermine support for his political rival in an upcoming election, also became a tool to prevent pastors from speaking out about politics from the pulpit.[1]

Johnson was not a fan of Senator Joseph McCarthy, nor his hearings and speeches about the growing threat of communism, and the voters in Texas hated communism and loved McCarthy. It turned out that tax-exempt organizations were funding Johnson's primary opponent, Dudley Dougherty, and funding anti-communist views through radio, television, books and magazines. Johnson had to use fraud to win his first senatorial election, but this time he had to do something to silence his opponent's supporters. A short amendment to the IRS code for regulating 501(c)(3) tax-exempt organizations would do just the trick.[2]

There was no debate on the amendment, and it was accepted on unanimous consent.[3]

The very idea of silencing religious leaders regarding political matters is unconstitutional. The 1st Amendment is clear, "Congress shall make no law...prohibiting the free exercise" of religion. The same goes for free speech.

As President of the United States, Johnson realized that the black vote could be a powerful voting block, if only they could be convinced to begin voting for Democrats. It was well known that Johnson was a racist,[4] as was the majority of his Democrat Party brethren.

President John Kennedy, after at first scarcely addressing racial issues during his first two years in office,[5] eventually decided it was time to pursue a civil rights bill like that of Republican President Eisenhower's Civil Rights Act of 1957. Sit-ins began occurring throughout the South, with some white supporters joining blacks. Robert Kennedy, the attorney general...called for a cooling-off period...[but more] incident[s] placed the president in the position of having to enforce federal laws against the will of a State.[6]   Robert Kennedy then sent troops in to preserve order…and by then JFK had proposed civil rights legislation to Congress, but the issues had been ignored too long.[7]   Kennedy found that no Democrat would work with him, so he had to recruit the help of the Republican Senate Minority Leader Everett Dirksen to resurrect the language proposed by Eisenhower's Attorney General in 1960, which later led to President Johnson signing into law the Civil Rights Act of 1964.[8]   When the Civil Rights Act of 1964 went to the two Houses of Congress for a vote, the Democrats tried to block the 1964 Civil Rights Act, and Congressional Republicans supported it in greater percentages than Democrats did.[9]

Lyndon B. Johnson, the racist, was concerned about the rise of black power. He knew he could not let the Republicans own civil rights, anymore. He said: "These Negroes, they're getting pretty uppity these days and that's a problem for us since they've got something now they never had before, the political pull to back up their uppityness. Now we've got to do something about this, we've got to give them a little something, just enough to quiet them down, not enough to make a difference. For if we don't move at all, then their allies will line up against us and there'll be no way of stopping them, we'll lose the filibuster and there'll be no way of putting a brake on all sorts of wild legislation.   It'll be Reconstruction all over again."[10]

Seven years later, President Johnson was working to "buy" and control the black vote via his Great Society programs, saying, "I'll have them ni**ers voting Democratic for two hundred years."[11]

Though the Republicans had been the primary force behind Civil Rights legislation, by signing the Civil Rights Act of 1964 President Johnson knew that he had earned the trust of the black community and if he played his political cards just right, he'd have them eating out of the hands of the Democrat Party's political machine. Unfortunately, The Great Society did more than pull the black community into the Democrat Party's new plantation through government dependency. It also created problems that would ultimately damage our country's economic and cultural well-being down the road.

When the mortgage bubble burst in 2009, as a member of the residential construction industry, I felt the pain early. The company I worked for instantly went from seven crews, six days a week to one crew, two days a week.

The birth and death of the housing bubble was directly associated with the games being played by the Federal Reserve, and various unconstitutional federal regulations (being created, and dismissed) regarding banking, insurance companies, and investment brokerages all the way back to Franklin Delano Roosevelt. While FDR began the madness, and Barack Obama took advantage of the situation, it was Lyndon B. Johnson's Great Society that really got the Democrats energized about supporting unconstitutional government-sponsored enterprises like Freddie Mac and Fannie Mae as vehicles to extend the Great Society initiatives.[12]

While the folks who oppose the U.S. Constitution will tell you that their desire for a more intrusive federal government is simply for the purpose of ensuring the common good, the reality is that the underlying goal is to increase political power, and do so through more control, which ultimately always leads to bondage.[13]

A master plan to oppose the *laissez faire* principles of the U.S. Constitution, which began with Alexander Hamilton, has grown in intensity over the last two and a half centuries. Its purpose is to move America away from its constitutional foundation towards socialism in a very slow, stealthy manner.

"The strategy is to promise the American people one thing and to deliver another. Never make it appear that you, the candidate, are supporting socialism or are a Socialist, even though the platforms you will support after your election are indeed socialist in nature. And you must never deliver so much socialism that the American people will discover the exact nature of the game and remove you from office."[14]

As a result of the creeping incrementalism towards

socialism, Americans have largely not caught on to what is going on, and have even gotten to the point that they have decided to welcome the promised enslavement. The latest generation views government as a good thing, freedom of speech as hate speech, and the Constitution as an oppressive document. The Great Society simply extended the plantation from the fields to a deeper position in the realm of politics, and the Democrats have convinced the oppressed that it's not only for their own good, but that without the tyranny they offer, the lowly worker class would be unable to fend for themselves against the evil, profit-mongering wealthy class.

Johnson realized early that if Americans could be convinced that to be dependent upon the federal government was a good thing, and that it was for their own good, they would come to the conclusion that they *should* be dependent upon the government. The intrusion of big government into our lives would be seen as proper and legitimate. Rather than the King's Realm, it is simply the Federal Government's Realm – a necessary development in the minds of the enslaved.

Frederick Douglass, a former slave, witnessed and described that exact phenomenon among his fellow slaves, many of whom were proud of how hard they worked for their masters and how faithfully they did as they were told. From their perspective, a runaway slave was a shameful thief, having 'stolen' himself from the master. Douglass described how thoroughly indoctrinated many slaves were, to the point where they truly believed that their own enslavement was just and righteous: "I have found that, to make a contented slave, it is necessary to make a thoughtless one. It is necessary to darken his moral and mental vision, and as far as possible, to annihilate the power of reason. He must be able to detect no inconsistencies in slavery; he must be made to feel that slavery is right; and he can be brought to that only when he ceases to be a man."[15]

The Democrats, through programs of government dependency, have been doing the exact same thing in modern times. The goal is collectivism, and individualism and humanity must be denied. The Khmer Rouge understood that to control people, their individuality and humanity must be erased, so that they become nothing more than dependants and loyalists to the state. "I am not a human being, I am an animal," can be read at the end of the confession of the former leader and minister Hu Nim. The implication was that a human life quite literally had no more value than that of a beast. People were killed for losing cattle and tortured to death for having struck a cow...Human life was worthless. "You have individual tendencies...You must...shed these illusions," Pin Yathay was told by one Khmer Rouge soldier when he attempted to keep his wounded son by his side..."You don't have a duty to help these people. On the contrary, that proves you still have pity and feelings of friendship. You must renounce such sentiments and wipe all such individualism from your mind."[16]

While the communist genocides committed by regimes in recent history are a far cry from what the Democrats are up to, the road to that kind of death toll by statism begins with a simple claim that government is there to help. The Founding Fathers viewed a centralized government as being a necessary evil, but recognized that if left unchecked, the potential for tyranny, bondage, and genocide was very real.

The presidency of Lyndon B. Johnson began after the assassination of President John F. Kennedy in November, 1963. President Johnson quickly engaged in an expansion of the powers of the federal government, signing an expansive slate of programs labeled as the Great Society, after he announced his domestic plans in May of 1964.

"In your time we have the opportunity to move not only toward the rich society and the powerful society, but upward to the Great Society. The Great Society rests on abundance and liberty for all. It demands an end to poverty and injustice, to which we are totally committed in our time."[17]

Fourteen task forces made up of academics and government experts studied American society: transportation, education, natural beauty, and civil rights. Every task force worked directly for the President. Their findings and recommendations were shared among government officials.[18]

The President has no legislative authorities, so Johnson submitted eighty-seven "suggested" bills to Congress. Congress passed eighty-four, and Johnson signed them all into law.[19]

Despite Johnson's reform measures, life for the nation's poor, particularly African Americans living in inner-city slums in the North, failed to show significant improvement. Vast numbers of African Americans still suffered from unemployment, run-down schools, and lack of adequate medical care, and many were malnourished or hungry. Expectations of prosperity arising from the promise of the Great Society failed to materialize, and discontent and alienation grew accordingly.[20]

Race relations worsened, as well. Division grew to the point that there were fears of a general "race war" in the air. The president responded by appointing a special panel to report on the crisis, the National Advisory Commission on Civil Disorders, which concluded that the country was in danger of dividing into two societies—one white, one black, "separate and unequal."[21]

While expanding the powers and scope of the federal government in a manner that was contrary to constitutional authorities granted, President Johnson claimed to be a defender of the U.S. Constitution. In his Proclamation #3786 on May 24, 1967, he indicated that "...the Constitution continues to guard fundamental rights...Our citizens—naturalized or native-born—must also seek to refresh and improve their knowledge of how our government operates under the Constitution and how they can participate in it. Only in this way can they assume the full responsibilities of citizenship and make our government more truly of, by, and for the people." He then designated the period beginning September 17 and ending September 23, 1967, as Constitution Week.[22]

On March 15, 1965, in a speech delivered before a joint session of Congress, President Johnson stated he spoke "for the dignity of man and the destiny of democracy."

Like his predecessors, and pretty much every politician since, he also called our system a democracy. Like his predecessors, he desired that America would become more democratic. Democracies are naturally transitional systems of government, and if the United States became a pure Democracy, it was assumed the socialist revolution would simply take place in the minds of the voters, and in the ballot boxes. No shot may ever need to be fired.

Johnson quoted Thomas Jefferson's penned words in the Declaration of Independence, and Patrick Henry's cry for liberty, in a speech to Congress. "'All men are created equal' — 'government by consent of the governed' — 'give me liberty or give me death.' Well, those are not just clever words, or those are not just empty theories. In their name Americans have fought and died for two centuries, and tonight around the world they stand there as guardians of our liberty, risking their lives."[23]

He went on later in his speech to summon the spirits of the Framers of the Constitution, again. "Our fathers believed that if this noble view of the rights of man was to flourish, it must be rooted in democracy. The most basic right of all was the right to choose your own leaders. The history of this country, in large measure, is the history of the expansion of that right to all of our people."[24]

He was attempting to appeal to those who supported the Civil Rights Movement because he was trying to drum up support for a Voter's Rights bill that was possible because of the recent ratification of the 24th Amendment. He hammered on the fact that "Every American citizen must have an equal right to vote. There is no reason which can excuse the denial of that right. There is no duty which weighs more heavily on us than the duty we have to ensure that right. Yet, the harsh fact is that in many places in this country, men and women are kept from voting simply because they are Negroes."[25]

While he was essentially right in what he was saying, based on the reality that he was a racist, one wonders if he meant what he was saying, or if it was simply motivated by political reasons.[26]

He next targeted the 15th Amendment. "In such a case our duty must be clear to all of us. The Constitution says that no person shall be kept from voting because of his race or his color. We have all sworn an oath before God to support and to defend that Constitution. We must now act in obedience to that oath…I will send to Congress a law designed to eliminate illegal barriers to the right to vote."[27]

After calling the federal government a "national government," Johnson turned his attention to the concept of States' Rights, a claim The South was still verbalizing. "There is no issue of States rights or national rights. There is only the struggle for human rights."[28]

He harkened back to Lincoln, but refused to name the Republican Party. "It was more than a hundred years ago that Abraham Lincoln, a great President of another party, signed the Emancipation Proclamation, but emancipation is a proclamation and not a fact. A century has passed, more than a hundred years, since equality was promised. And yet the Negro is not equal. A century has passed since the day of promise. And the promise is unkept."[29]

Why would a President claiming to be a champion for the Constitution, and claiming to believe in Civil Rights, usurp the Constitution and attempt to create a system that ultimately expanded government dependency, and destroyed the family unit in the Black Community?

Johnson's "War on Poverty" has only resulted in a ballooning of government spending at every level of government. Reports indicate[30] that there is little to show for the massive amount of taxpayer dollars being transferred to those below the poverty line as the poverty rate ticks upward each year. A report from Michael Tanner of the Cato Institute showed that "Since President Lyndon B. Johnson first declared a "war on poverty" in 1964, federal, state and local governments have spent roughly $15 trillion fighting poverty. In constant dollars, federal spending on welfare and anti-poverty programs has jumped from $178 billion to $668 billion over the past 47 years — a 375 percent increase in constant 2011 dollars. Total welfare spending — including state and local funds — has increased from $256 billion to $908 billion, a 355 percent increase."[31]

The federal government operates 126 programs aimed at tackling poverty in the hopes that people will improve their situation with a little help from the government. Instead of poverty being eradicated as bloviating politicians routinely insist will happen if just a few more programs are better funded, more people are taking government benefits than ever before.[32]

Johnson's programs have been doing exactly the opposite of what they claimed they would do, and instead of eliminating poverty, it has not only increased at an alarming rate, but so has the size and scope of the power of the federal government.

▶ In 1960 only 22% of families in the black community were single-parent households.
In 2017, that number was at about 72%.[33]

▶ According to the 1938 Encyclopaedia of the Social Sciences, in 1938 about 11% of black children were born to unwed mothers. Today about 75% of black children are born to unwed mothers.[34]

▶ Two-parent black families are rarely poor. Only 8% of black married-couple families live in poverty. Among black families in which both the husband and wife work full time, the poverty rate is under 5%. Poverty in black families headed by single women is 37%. As early as 1900, when racism was rampant, the duration of black unemployment was 15 percent shorter than that of whites. Today, during a time where we just finished two terms of the first black President, and experienced the candidacy of a black neurosurgeon named Ben Carson in the 2016 election for the White House, it's about 30 percent longer.[35]

According to the Heritage Foundation, "The effect of married fathers on child outcomes can be quite pronounced. For example, examination of families with the same race and same parental education shows that, compared with intact married families, children from single-parent homes are:

☐ More than twice as likely to be arrested for a juvenile crime.
☐ Twice as likely to be treated for emotional and behavioral problems.
☐ Roughly twice as likely to be suspended or expelled from school.
☐ A third more likely to drop out before completing high school.[36]

The effects of being raised in a single-parent home continue into adulthood. Comparing families of the same race and similar incomes, children from broken and single-parent homes are three times more likely to end up in jail by the time they reach age 30 than are children raised in intact married families. Compared with girls raised in similar married families, girls from single-parent homes are more than twice as likely to have a child without being married, thereby repeating the negative cycle for another generation.[37]

The decline of marriage contributes to declining self-sufficiency and increased official poverty in future generations. Children living in single-parent homes are 50 percent more likely to experience official poverty as adults when compared with children from intact married homes. This intergenerational poverty effect persists even after adjusting for the original differences in family income and poverty during childhood.[38]

Throughout U.S. history, marriage was the norm. Prior to the mid-1960s, nearly all children were born to married couples. When the War on Poverty began in 1964, only 7 percent of children were born to unmarried women. However, over the next four-and-a-half decades the share of non-marital births exploded. In 2013, 41 percent of all children born in the U.S. were born outside marriage.[39]

The reality is two-fold. One, the problems that exist in the black community are not the result of racism or police brutality, but instead is directly related to the breakdown of the family unit. Two, the breakdown of the family unit began to occur at about the same time as President Johnson kicked the welfare system into high gear. The Democrat Party remains to be the party of government dependency. Under the presidency of Barack Obama, by 2012 (only halfway through his presidency, mind you) federal spending on welfare programs increased by 32%. The number of able-bodied adults on food stamps doubled from 1.9 million in 2008 to 3.9 million in 2010.[40]

What Johnson launched was a war on the family, a dehumanizing strategy that discounts individualism, and morality, in the same way the communists do. The thing is, the U.S. Constitution does not grant to the federal government the authority to be involved in any of the war-on-poverty programs. The destruction of the family unit, and American Liberty, is being accomplished against the original intent of the U.S. Constitution.

As Benjamin Franklin so wisely said, "Only a virtuous people are capable of freedom. As nations become corrupt and vicious, they have more need of masters."[41] With an unwillingness to keep the family together, and a refusal to break away from receiving gifts from the treasury of government (which kills incentive), how can the percentage of blacks who remain in poverty ever expect to change their own conditions? And the bigger question is, as these policies continue to expand, how long until all Americans are ensnared by them?

The legacy of President Johnson, regardless of his claims of wanting to protect the Constitution, and despite his words of unity, screams loudly of division, and an unconstitutional expansion of the powers of the federal government. Like the socialists and communists, he claimed to have the best of intentions. The reality is that Johnson was not only an enemy of the Constitution, but the effects of his unconstitutional activities are still being felt today, from his incentive killing welfare programs, his failed war on poverty, and yes, even the collapse of the mortgage bubble in 2009.

• 7: Barack Obama

In 1995, Barack Obama was teaching constitutional law as a University of Chicago adjunct professor.[1]

The University of Chicago website states, "From 1992 until his election to the U.S. Senate in 2004, Barack Obama served as a professor in the Law School. He was a Lecturer from 1992 to 1996. He was a Senior Lecturer from 1996 to 2004, during which time he taught three courses per year. Senior Lecturers are considered to be members of the Law School faculty and are regarded as professors, although not full-time or tenure-track. The title of Senior Lecturer is distinct from the title of Lecturer, which signifies adjunct status. Like Obama, each of the Law School's Senior Lecturers have high-demand careers in politics or public service, which prevent full-time teaching. Several times during his 12 years as a professor in the Law School, Obama was invited to join the faculty in a full-time tenure-track position, but he declined."[2]

President Obama taught "Con Law III" at Chicago...Con Law III covers the 14th Amendment.[3]

One former student called Obama's ignorance of the U.S. Constitution, "Embarrassing."[4]

I do not believe it was ignorance, as much as it was disapproval, of the basic principles of the United States Constitution by Barack Obama, that fueled the comment by the student regarding Obama's constitutional positions. Based on comments by Barack Obama, he fully understands the original intent of the U.S. Constitution, but finds it to be an obstacle to the political plans his leftist ideology maintains. Therefore, as did his constitutional liar predecessors, he sought to use case law and the concept of implied powers to circumvent constitutional authority.

The 14th Amendment is the second of three Reconstruction Amendments ratified after the War Between the States. Among all constitutional amendments, one can easily argue that the fourteenth is the one that is misapplied as originally intended, the most. From the 14th Amendment we have, as a modern society, grossly misinterpreted regularly the Citizenship Clause, the Due Process Clause and the Equal Protection Clause. Case Law has grabbed a hold of those clauses and has twisted them to the point that they are no longer recognizable.

Questions surrounding the 14th Amendment made up the subject taught by senior lecturer Barack Obama at the University of Chicago Law School...[Obama] taught rights, race and gender...his most popular course, the political and historical seminar titled "Current Issues in Racism and Law," offered in 2004, corroborates...observation that "Mr. Obama improvised his own textbook...."[5]

Noni Elison-Southall recalled that she enrolled in Obama's "Current Issues in Racism and the Law" because she wanted to further her understanding of the themes that dominated the race debate in the United States and the laws that emerged from it. In a school where discussions about race and law didn't always feel welcome, Obama's class provided a safe haven, in her opinion, to analyze and discuss the complexity and diversity of opinions around racial gerrymandering, race and the criminal justice system and affirmative action. She says his class was hard work. She remembered leaving his class intellectually and emotionally drained.[6]

Obama's journey to the University of Chicago is an odd one. The journey from Columbia University to Editor of the Harvard Law Review to an appointment on the University of Chicago faculty is typically littered with scholarly publications, clerkships and other professional accolades. In Obama's case, the most conspicuous items on his resume were two autobiographies — both about his racial identity — and an unremarkable stint in Illinois politics.[7]

Shortly after Barack Obama was elected President of the United States, I was at a car repair shop waiting for my vehicle to have some work done on it. In the lobby I struck up a conversation with a young man, and during our verbal intercourse I stated that I was teaching Constitution classes at the local gun shop on Thursday Nights. A woman, who had been listening in on our dialogue, piped up and said, "Well, if you teach the Constitution, then you must be very happy about the fact that we just elected a Constitutional Law Professor as President."

I responded, "His version of the Constitution is not the same as originally intended. And, from my reading, I have determined that what he taught was not Constitutional Law, but how to use the 14th Amendment to create racial division."

My assertion was largely based on Obama's history before he arrived at the University of Chicago as a lecturer.

From the mid to late 1980s, Barack Obama worked as a community organizer in Chicago. According to Hoover Institution Fellow and economist Thomas Sowell, "For community organizers...racial resentments are a stock in trade...what [they] organize are the resentments and paranoia within a community, directing those feelings against other communities, from whom either benefits or revenge are to be gotten, using whatever rhetoric or tactics will accomplish that purpose."[8]

Saul Alinsky wrote, "[The community organizer] must first rub raw the resentments of the people; fan the latent hostilities to the point of overt expression. He must search out controversy and issues, rather than avoid them, for unless there is controversy people are not concerned enough to act[9a].... [His function is] to agitate to the point of conflict.... Pick the target, freeze it, personalize it, and polarize it[9b] .... [T]here is no point to tactics unless one has a target upon which to center the attacks."[9c]

In the early to mid-1990s, Obama worked with the (now defunct) community organization ACORN and its voter-mobilization arm, "Project Vote." In 2003, Manhattan Institute scholar Sol Stern wrote that ACORN, professing a dedication to "the poor and powerless," in fact "promotes a 1960s-bred agenda of anti-capitalism, central planning, victimology, and government handouts to the poor." ACORN, Stern elaborated, organized people "to push for ever more government control of the economy," and to pursue "the ultra-Left's familiar anti-capitalist redistributionism."[10]

Obama's anti-constitution adherence to communist ideas of the redistribution of wealth was verbalized by him October 19, 1998, when he said at a conference at Loyola University, "There has been a systematic...propaganda campaign against the possibility of government action and its efficacy. And I think some of it has been deserved.... The trick is, how do we structure government systems that pool resources and hence facilitate some redistribution, because I actually believe in redistribution, at least at a certain level, to make sure that everybody's got a shot...To the extent that we are doing research figuring out what kinds of government action would successfully make their [the working poor's] lives better, we are then putting together a potential majority coalition to move those agendas forward."[11]

On October 6, 2011 Obama congratulated, during a press conference, the subversive activities of the anti-capitalist Occupy Wall Street activists for "express[ing] the frustrations that the American people feel...about how our financial system works"; for reminding him "what we are still fighting for"; for "inspir[ing]" him; and for being "the reason why I ran for this office in the first place."[12]

On July 13, 2012, Obama minimized the achievements of entrepreneurs, and emphasized the notion that government was the key to a thriving economy: "Look, if you've been successful, you didn't get there on your own. You didn't get there on your own. I'm always struck by people who think, 'well, it must be because I was just so smart.' There are a lot of smart people out there. 'It must be because I worked harder than everybody else.' Let me tell you something—there are a whole bunch of hardworking people out there. If you were successful, somebody along the line gave you some help.... Somebody invested in roads and bridges. If you've got a business—you didn't build that. Somebody else made that happen. The Internet didn't get invented on its own. Government research created the Internet so that all the companies could make money off the Internet."[13]

In a January 23, 2015 interview with Ezra Klein of Vox, President Obama said that traditional market forces that historically redistributed income were failing, and that the time for government to take on that role had thus arrived. At one point in the interview, Klein asked: "To focus a bit on that long-term question, does that put us in a place where redistribution becomes, in a sense, a positive good in and of itself? Do we need the government playing the role not of powering the growth engine — which is a lot of what had to be done after the financial crisis — but of making sure that while that growth engine is running, it is ensuring that enough of the gains and prosperity is shared so that the political support for that fundamental economic model remains strong?"[14]

Obama replied, "That's always been the case. I don't think that's entirely new. The fact of the matter is that relative to our post-war history, taxes now are not particularly high or particularly progressive compared to what they were, say, in the late '50s or the '60s. And there's always been this notion that for a country to thrive there are some things, as Lincoln says, that we can do better together than we can do for ourselves. And whether that's building roads, or setting up effective power grids, or making sure that we've got high-quality public education — that teachers are paid enough — the market will not cover those things. And we've got to do them together. Basic research falls in that category. So that's always been true.[15]

"I think that part of what's changed is that a lot of that burden for making sure that the pie was broadly shared took place before government even got involved. If you had stronger unions, you had higher wages. If you had a corporate culture that felt a sense of place and commitment so that the CEO was in Pittsburgh or was in Detroit and felt obliged, partly because of social pressure but partly because they felt a real affinity toward the community, to re-invest in that community and to be seen as a good corporate citizen. Today what you have is quarterly earning reports, compensation levels for CEOs that are tied directly to those quarterly earnings. You've got international capital that is demanding maximizing short-term profits. And so what happens is that a lot of the distributional questions that used to be handled in the marketplace through decent wages or health care or defined benefit pension plans — those things all are eliminated. And the average employee, the average worker, doesn't feel any benefit.[16]

"So part of our job is, what can government do directly through tax policy? What we've proposed, for example, in terms of capital gains — that would make a big difference in our capacity to give a tax break to a working mom for child care. And that's smart policy, and there's no evidence that would hurt the incentives of folks at Google or Microsoft or Uber not to invent what they invent or not to provide services they provide. It just means that instead of $20 billion, maybe they've got 18, right? But it does mean that Mom can go to work without worrying that her kid's not in a safe place.[17]

"We also still have to focus on the front end. Which is even before taxes are paid, are there ways that we can increase the bargaining power: making sure that an employee has some measurable increases in their incomes and their wealth and their security as a consequence of an economy that's improving. And that's where issues like labor laws make a difference. That's where say in shareholder meetings and trying to change the culture in terms of compensation at the corporate level could make a difference. And there's been some interesting conversations globally around issues like inclusive capitalism and how we can make it work for everybody."[18]

Obama also said that policymakers must "make sure" that "folks at the very top are doing enough of their fair share," and he disparaged the "winner-take-all aspect of this modern economy" and the need to be "investing enough in the common good."[19]

Ezra Klein's interview with Barack Obama revealed the President's deep support for Marxist concepts such as a redistribution of wealth and government intrusion into all aspects of the economic system, all of which carry with them allegiance to collectivism, or as Hillary Clinton would call it, "It takes a Village."[20]

In short, when wages or benefits are driven upward by force through union threats or government intervention, it hurts the overall economic picture. When wages and benefits rise due to natural free market forces, it contributes to the overall economic picture, and produces ripples of prosperity that reaches all participants in the financial picture.

In an interview published by the Daily Herald on March 3, 1990, Harvard Law School student Barack Obama said, "There's certainly racism here [at Harvard Law School]. There are certain burdens that are placed [on blacks], more emotionally at this point than concretely.... Hopefully, more and more people will begin to feel their story is somehow part of this larger story of how we're going to reshape America in a way that is less *mean-spirited* and more generous. I mean, I really hope to be part of a transformation of this country."[21]

For two decades, Jeremiah Wright was Barack

Obama's pastor and spiritual mentor in Chicago. So great was Obama's regard for Wright, that Obama selected him not only to perform his wedding to Michelle Robinson in 1992, but also to baptize his two daughters later on. Wright's many writings, public statements, and sermons reflect his conviction that America has historically been an evil nation, infested with racism, prejudice, and injustices that have created a living hell for nonwhite people domestically and abroad. From Wright's point of view, America was founded on racism, and that is how the country is still run.[22]

Obama's own racism was exposed when a photograph at a Congressional Black Caucus (CBC) meeting in 2005 emerged, showing a smiling Obama posing with the anti-Semitic black nationalist Louis Farrakhan. The photographer, Nation Of Islam employee Askia Muhammad, subsequently hid the photo for the next 13 years, in order to protect Obama politically. As Muhammad explained in January 2018, he had "basically swor[n] secrecy" and handed over the picture to Farrakhan's chief of staff and son-in-law, Leonard Farrakhan, who had kept the photo hidden for 13 years.[23]

A Judicial Watch investigation revealed that federal funding for the often violent, and very racist, National Council of La Raza and its affiliates skyrocketed after President Obama had appointed La Raza's senior vice president, Cecilia Muñoz, to be his director of intergovernmental affairs in 2009.

The year Muñoz joined the White House, government funds earmarked for La Raza increased from $4.1 million to $11 million. Fully 60% of that money came from the Department of Labor, headed by Hilda Solis, who has close ties to the La Raza movement. Also in 2010, the Department of Housing and Urban Development gave La Raza $2.5 million for housing counseling, the Department of Education contributed almost $800,000, and the Centers for Disease Control gave approximately $250,000.[24]

Sowing the seeds of division between the races was not enough for Obama, however, so in 2011 he began his campaign of sowing the seeds of division between blacks and law enforcement. On May 31, 2011, it was reported that "President Obama's Justice Department is aggressively investigating several big urban police departments for systematic civil rights abuses such as harassment of racial minorities, false arrests, and excessive use of force...."[25]

The Ferguson riot emerged after Obama falsely accused Missouri's law enforcement of racial bias. On March 4, 2015, Obama's Department of Justice (DOJ) released an 87-page report stating conclusively that based on physical and eyewitness evidence, Officer Darren Wilson's fatal shooting of Michael Brown in Ferguson, Missouri (in August 2014) was justified; that Wilson's version of events was consistent with the physical and eyewitness evidence; and that just prior to the shooting, Brown in fact had assaulted Wilson, tried to steal his gun, and charged at him in an effort to harm or kill him. Notwithstanding these facts, President Obama, in the days that followed, announced that the Ferguson Police Department was awash in racism and discrimination against African Americans. Said Obama at a town hall-style meeting in South Carolina: "What we saw was that the Ferguson Police Department in conjunction with the municipality saw traffic stops, arrests, tickets as a revenue generator, as opposed to serving the community, and that it systematically was biased against African Americans in that city who were stopped, harassed, mistreated, abused, called names, fined."[26]

Obama lied, disagreeing with his own Department of Justice's report, for the purpose to stir discontent and create racial division and violence – and he succeeded. The Justice Department later came out with a new report, one that was in more agreement with the President.[27]

In April 2015, according to a Defense Department-approved "sexism course" prepared by the Defense Equal Opportunity Management Institute (DEOMI), – an entity whose mission is to provide a "world-class human relations education" – the Bible, the U.S. Constitution, and the Declaration of Independence are all "historical influences that allow sexism and racism to continue."[28]

By the end of his presidency, two things were clear; Barack Obama's agenda of creating racial division was working, and the dismantling of what remained of constitutional America was in full swing.

It turned out that Obama's disdain for the U.S. Constitution shouldn't have been a surprise.

A 2001 interview of then Senator Barack Obama revealed that the President to be saw the Constitution as being a document with a list of inadequacies. He said, during the interview, that the Constitution is merely "a charter of negative liberties. It says what the states can't do to you. Says what the federal government can't do to you, but doesn't say what the federal government or state government must do on your behalf."[29]

He was disappointed that the Constitution did not contain a plan for "redistributive change." Obama was unhappy with the constraints of our Constitution, and the restraints it put on the federal government. He, like his fellow Democrats, have verbalized often their position that the courts may interpret the law, and the U.S. Constitution, to mean whatever they want, and that rights are not natural and God-given, but are created by government, where they are then guaranteed, administered, and subsidized if necessary. Not only can government create rights, according to Obama, but they can also take them away.

Like his progressive predecessors, Obama also believed that the President of the United States was entitled to take "independent action" when he felt it necessary. He issued 39 executive orders in 2009; 35 in 2010; 34 in 2011; 39 in 2012; 20 in 2013; 31 in 2014; 29 in 2015; 43 in 2016; and 7 "midnight" executive orders in January of 2017 right before the inauguration of President Donald Trump.[30] Barack Obama's total number of executive orders while in office was 276, *technically* slightly less than every president since John F. Kennedy (save for Gerald Ford and George Herbert Walker Bush).

In 2014, the criticism against President Obama's use of executive orders became so extreme that he felt the need to address the issue during a speech on July 10, 2014 at the audience at the Paramount Theatre in Austin, Texas, "The truth is, even with all the actions I've taken this year, I'm issuing executive orders at the lowest rate in more than 100 years. So it's not clear how it is that Republicans didn't seem to mind when President Bush took more executive actions than I did."[31]

The truth is, Obama was lying. Obama realized he could take many executive actions under the radar. As 2014 dawned, frustrated that the Republican Congress was not bending to his every whim and will, Obama said, "We're not just going to be waiting for legislation in order to make sure that we're providing Americans the kind of help they need. I've got a pen and I've got a phone, and I can use that pen to sign executive orders and take executive actions and administrative actions that move the ball forward."[32]

What Obama was referring to were executive memos, executive letters, and executive actions. Unlike executive orders, memos, letters, and actions are not numbered. In fact, some of them are not even revealed to the general public or the media.

USA Today, in an article titled, "Obama Issues 'Executive Orders by Another Name", published December 16, 2014, author Gregory Korte explained, "President Obama has issued a form of executive action known as the presidential memorandum more often than any other president in history — using it to take unilateral action even as he has signed fewer executive orders...Obama is on track to take more high-level executive actions than any president since Harry Truman...Like executive orders, presidential memoranda don't require action by Congress. They have the same force of law [*force of law? I thought only Congress possessed legislative powers?*] as executive orders and often have consequences just as far-reaching. And some of the most significant actions of the Obama presidency have come not by executive order but by presidential memoranda...Obama has made prolific use of memoranda despite his own claims that he's used his executive power less than other presidents...Obama has issued 195 executive orders as of Tuesday [December 9, 2014]. Published alongside them in the Federal Register are 198 presidential memoranda — all of which carry the same legal force as executive orders. He's already signed 33% more presidential memoranda in less than six years than Bush did in eight. He's also issued 45% more than the last Democratic president, Bill Clinton, who assertively used memoranda to signal what kinds of regulations he wanted federal agencies to adopt. Obama is not the first president to use memoranda to accomplish policy aims. But at this point in his presidency, he's the first to use them more often than executive orders...even as he's quietly used memoranda to signal policy changes to federal agencies, Obama and his allies have claimed he's been more restrained in his use of that power...In a Senate floor speech in July [2014], Majority Leader Harry Reid said, 'While Republicans accuse President Obama of executive overreach, they neglect the fact that he has issued far fewer executive orders than any two-term president in the last 50 years.'...'There is no question that this president has been judicious in his use of executive action, executive orders, and I think those numbers thus far have come in below what President George W. Bush and President Bill Clinton did,' said Jay Carney, then the White House press secretary, in February [2014]...While executive orders have become a kind of Washington shorthand for unilateral presidential action, presidential memoranda have gone largely unexamined. And yet memoranda are often as significant to everyday Americans than executive orders...Two...recent memos directed the administration to coordinate an overhaul of the nation's immigration system — a move that congressional Republicans say exceeded his authority...Memoranda are not numbered, not indexed and, until recently, difficult to quantify. Kenneth Lowande, a political science doctoral student at the University of Virginia, counted up memoranda published in the Code of Federal Regulations since 1945. In an article published in the December issue of Presidential Studies Quarterly, he found that memoranda appear to be replacing executive orders...'If you look at some of the titles of memoranda recently, they do look like and mirror executive orders,' Lowande said. The difference may be one of political messaging, he said. An 'executive order,' he said, 'immediately evokes potentially damaging questions of imperial overreach.' Memorandum sounds less threatening...[Supreme Court Justice Elena] Kagan said Clinton considered memoranda 'a central part of his governing strategy,' using them to spur agencies to write regulations restricting tobacco advertising to children, allowing unemployment insurance for paid family leave and requiring agencies to collect racial profiling data. The memoranda became, ever increasingly over the course of eight years, Clinton's primary means, self-consciously undertaken, both of setting an administrative agenda that reflected and advanced his policy and political preferences and of ensuring the execution of this program."[33]

"Presidential scholar Phillip Cooper calls

presidential memoranda 'executive orders by another name, and yet unique.' The law does not define the difference between an executive order and a memorandum, but it does say that the president should publish in the Federal Register executive orders and other documents that 'have general applicability and legal effect.' Something that's in a presidential memorandum in one administration might be captured in an executive order in another,' said Jim Hemphill, the special assistant to the director for the government's legal notice publication. 'There's no guidance that says, 'Mr. President, here's what needs to be in an executive order.'"[34]

"There are subtle differences. Executive orders are numbered; memoranda are not. Memoranda are always published in the Federal Register after proclamations and executive orders. And under Executive Order 11030, signed by President Kennedy in 1962, an executive order must contain a 'citation of authority,' saying what law it's based on. Memoranda have no such requirement."[35]

For Obama, the use of executive memorandums accomplished two deeds he desired. It quelled his critics who were accusing him of using too many executive orders, and it allowed him to do as he pleased without having to worry about providing any citation of authority.

As with Theodore Roosevelt, Obama believed in the

concept of a strong executive, using executive orders, memos, letters and actions to perform anything he wanted not specifically prohibited by the Constitution, from his point of view.

Jay Carney, while critical of Bush's executive actions, argued in Obama's favor by saying it wasn't the number of executive actions that was important but rather "the quality and the type."

"It is funny to hear Republicans get upset about the suggestion that the president might use legally available authorities to advance an agenda that expands opportunity and rewards hard work and responsibility, when obviously they supported a president who used executive authorities quite widely," he said.[36]

The Affordable Care Act (Obamacare) was modified a number of times through executive power. The law was passed March of 2010, and signaling his willingness to "go it alone," acting without congressional approval, Obama issued a number of executive orders in defiance of the President's statutory or constitutional authority.

Obamacare was originally written to generally require that businesses employing 50 or more full-time employees provide health insurance or pay a fine per each uncovered employee. Section 1513(d) of the law provided that this employer mandate provision "shall apply to months beginning after

December 31, 2013." Yet, in response to complaints from the business community that this requirement was too burdensome, on July 2, 2013, the Obama Administration announced that enforcement of the employer mandate would be delayed until January 2015.[37]

A modification of any law can only be performed by Congress because in Article I, Section 1 of the United States Constitution the document instructs that "all Legislative Power...shall be vested in a Congress of the United States." Therefore, the President has no constitutional authority to modify the law in any way, including pushing back the employer mandate's effective date.

Additionally, the Office of Personnel Management issued a proposed rule to allow Members of Congress and their staffs to receive generous taxpayer-funded premium support. Congress explicitly considered and rejected proposed amendments to Obamacare that would have created a specific allowance for a congressional health care subsidy; indeed, such an exemption seems inconsistent with the congressional decision not to provide for such a subsidy under Section 1312(d)(3)(D) of the law, which explicitly states that "[n]otwithstanding any other provision of law...the only health plans that the Federal Government may make available to Members of Congress and congressional staff shall be health plans that are" created under Obamacare or offered through an

Obamacare exchange.[38]

Congress could have fixed the problem by amending the law, but instead, the Obama Administration opted to unconstitutionally stretch the law to save Obamacare—at the taxpayers' expense.[39]

On November 14, 2013, the Administration announced in a letter to insurance commissioners that for one year, it would decline to enforce certain Obamacare requirements against insurance companies offering non-compliant plans and encouraged state insurance commissioners not to enforce the law as well. The letter announcing this non-enforcement had no basis in law, and the President threatened to veto legislation that would codify and authorize the one-year extension.[40]

Making law through his executive powers was not the only unconstitutional actions by President Obama. January 2012, President Obama made four "recess" appointments to the National Labor Relations Board (NLRB) and Consumer Financial Protection Bureau, claiming that, since the Senate was conducting only periodic pro forma sessions, it was not available to confirm those appointees. Yet the Senate was not in "the Recess," and a three-judge panel of the D.C. Circuit struck down the appointments to the NLRB as unconstitutional in *Noel Canning v. NLRB*. That court reasoned that the Recess Appointments Clause is not an alternative to Senate confirmation and "serve[s] only as a stopgap for times when the Senate was unable to provide advice and consent."[41]

The constitutional deficiency of these appointments is only the beginning of the problem. Once on the NLRB, the "recess" appointees rubber-stamped a number of questionable policies, such as requiring employers to post a list of "worker rights" (invalidated by two federal appellate courts) and snap elections for union representations. The illegitimate board also encouraged unionization by "card check," which has employees publicly sign membership cards, even though NLRB member Nancy Schiffer stated that she believes the board lacks the authority to mandate card check.[42]

Article II, Section 2 of the Constitution provides that the President may "fill up all Vacancies that may happen during the Recess of the Senate." Otherwise, the President must receive the advice and consent (confirmation) by the Senate for ambassadors, judges, and higher-level executive officers.

The Obama administration also abandoned its defense of laws in court, and issued expansive waivers to existing laws.[43]

Barack Obama, and his team of progressives, circumvented the constitutional authority that grants the House of Representatives the "purse strings" of federal revenue and spending the moment the idea for another stimulus package floated by their power-hungry gazes.

The stimulus package was not earmarked in the same manner that budgetary funds normally are. In a budget, receipts, budget authority, and outlays are all discussed, prepared, and managed. Budget earmarks cover two general kinds of spending. *Mandatory* spending covers entitlement programs, such as food stamps, Social Security, and agricultural subsidies. Mandatory spending may not be limited in the appropriations process. *Discretionary* spending is set annually in the appropriations process.

The stimulus package (like omnibus bills), however, was a whole new animal, and it was designed to be so on purpose. The claim by the establishment is that if it is not named a budget, then different rules apply. The Constitution's requirement is that only the House of Representatives (the only part of government that serves as the people's voice from the point of view of original intent and foundational construction of the document) may appropriate funds for specific targets. So, the executive branch's hands are tied when it comes to unwieldy spending. The President cannot spend federal funds without authority granted by Congress. Many of President Obama's plans, or should I say the "Democrat Party's and Global Establishment's plans", included expenditures that Obama knew may not earn the approval of Congress, and were definitely not the kind of expenditures Obama and his allies wanted to be discussed in the media or in the court of public opinion. The Obama administration wanted to be able to access a pile of funds that was unmonitored, and uncontrolled, by outside sources.

President Obama sent money to feed his leftist desires, while claiming they were for stimulating the economy. Wisconsin received $701 million in funding in the guise of saving the State from catastrophe. $600 million of those funds, or 80% of the overall funds that went to Wisconsin from President Obama's 2009 stimulus package, were dumped into the coffers of public unions. The move did not save Wisconsin – it saved the Democrat dominated unions. Once the unions' pockets were lined with federal funds from Obama's stimulus package slush fund, they proceeded to try and use those millions of those dollars to oust Wisconsin's Republican Governor, Scott Walker, from office.[44]

Walker miraculously survived the recall effort, and then proceeded to complete his conservative strategies, which has since pulled Wisconsin from the throes of death, and in the 2018 "Quality of Life Rankings", Wisconsin ranked number three. Liberal Democrat dominated California rounded out the list at number fifty.[45]

Obama's money-placement strategy was repeated over and over, with money going to the unions in Detroit, California, and ultimately places that Americans would never have dreamed "stimulus money" would ever wind up – such as the $1.7

billion to Iran, made entirely in cash. The Obama administration claimed the payment was the settlement of a decades-old arbitration claim between the United States and Iran. The funds, according to the Obama White House, came from a little-known fund administered by the Treasury Department for settling litigation claims. The so-called Judgment Fund is taxpayer money Congress has permanently approved in the event it's needed, allowing the president to bypass direct congressional approval to make a settlement. The U.S. previously paid out $278 million in Iran-related claims by using the fund in 1991.[46] It is likely the money that went to Iran was a mixture of the Judgment Fund and stimulus money. The Obama administration, however, covered its tracks so well, we may never know exactly where that money went. A whopping $162 million in stimulus funds wound up unaccounted for.[47]

It was the ultimate *redistribution of wealth* scheme, providing Obama's allies, the Democrat Party machine (which includes the unions), and Iran with a massive infusion of much-needed money that was not going to appear otherwise – which in the end not only fueled the progressive political apparatus so that it may continue to be a benefit to the Obama regime, but the funds also saved Iran from an impending economic collapse.

In short, Obama's Democrats confiscated the people's money through taxes, and then passed that money to the far reaches of the leftist global system so that they may use it in their war against liberty, the U.S. Constitution, and patriots who participate in the fight.

Rush Limbaugh referred to the stimulus bill as being "nothing more than a money laundering slush fund" through which a large portion of the money just goes right back to the Democrat party.[48]

My response to that woman at the automobile repair shop who asked me about my feelings regarding a constitutional professor being elected President of the United States was a shock to her. I said that "Obama's anti-American and anti-Constitution belief system is hardly what I would expect from a so-called constitutional law professor. Then again, if he truly understood the U.S. Constitution, and its definitions, he would also have known that he was not eligible for the office of the President of the United States in the first place; not because of where his birth certificate says he was born, but because according to the definition of Natural Born Citizen at the time of the writing of the Constitution, it was clear that to be eligible to be a candidate for the President of the United States one needed to have both parents as citizens of the United States at the time of birth of the child."[49]

Barack Obama was not eligible to be President of the United States. He was not a defender of the U.S. Constitution. And, as it turned out that, he was just another Constitutional Liar.

• Postscript: Abraham Lincoln

When I discuss Abraham Lincoln, I like to begin with, "I think he was a good man in a very unenviable position." The reality is that he was also a product of his time. As a young lawyer he had been schooled in the legal theories that were based on John Marshall's philosophies. Judicial review, thus judicial interpretation of the U.S. Constitution, was a common understanding in the legal world when Abraham Lincoln decided to pursue law.

John Marshall died on July 6, 1835 in Philadelphia.[1] In 1834 Abraham Lincoln began his political career and was elected to the Illinois state legislature as a member of the Whig Party. It was also around this time that he decided to become a lawyer, teaching himself the law by reading William Blackstone's Commentaries on the Laws of England. After being admitted to the bar in 1837, he moved to Springfield, Illinois, and began to practice in the John T. Stuart law firm.[2]

Lincoln called his move to Springfield his "experiment" in law.[3] During his time in Springfield, Lincoln began to attract the circle of friends and admirers who would play a decisive role in his political ascent. While he worked during the day to build his law practice, evenings would find him in the center of Springfield's young men, gathering around a fire in [Joshua Fry] Speed's store to read newspapers, gossip, and engage in philosophical debates.[4] "It was sort of a social club," Speed observed. Whigs and Democrats alike gathered to discuss the events of the day. Among the members of this "club" were three future U.S. senators: Stephen Douglas, who would become Lincoln's principal rival; Edward Baker, who would introduce him at his first inaugural and become one of the first casualties of the Civil War; and Orville Browning, who would assist his fight for the presidential nomination.[5]

As a young legislator in the Illinois legislature, while the rise of abolitionism in the North and the actions of governors, such as [William H.] Seward [of New York], who refused to fully respect the fugitive slave provisions in the Constitution, led legislatures in both South and North to pass resolutions that censured abolitionism and confirmed the [constitution's protections of] slavery, in conservative Illinois, populated by many citizens of Southern birth, the general assembly fell in line. By the lopsided vote of 77-6, the assembly resolved that "we highly disapprove of the formation of abolition societies," hold "sacred the "right of property in slaves," and believe that "the General Government cannot abolish slavery in the District of Columbia, against the consent of the citizens." Lincoln was among the six dissenting voices.[6]

Constitutionally, the U.S. Congress could abolish slavery in the District of Columbia, as per Article I, Section 8 of the U.S. Constitution (To exercise exclusive Legislation in all Cases whatsoever, over such District), and Article IV., Section 3 (The Congress shall have Power to dispose of and make all needful Rules and Regulations respecting the Territory or other Property belonging to the United States).

Lincoln was participating in the political system at a time immediately following Andrew Jackson's call for democracy and a firm union of States, and immediately following John Marshall's very long stint as Chief Justice of the United States where interpretation of the Constitution, including whether or not the Constitution is "just", by the courts was the common theme of discussion. He had spent his early years trying to decipher the meaning of the Declaration of Independence,[7] and he had a "lifelong quest to become an educated person."[8]

Through it all, Lincoln thought of himself as the heir to the Hamiltonian political tradition, which sought a more centralized governmental system.[9] Lincoln claimed to love and cherish the United States Constitution as he approached his presidency:[10]

- "Don't interfere with anything in the Constitution. That must be maintained, for it is the only safeguard of our liberties. And not to Democrats alone do I make this appeal, but to all who love these great and true principles." -- August 27, 1856 Speech at Kalamazoo, Michigan

- "Let us then turn this government back into the channel in which the framers of the Constitution originally placed it." -- July 10, 1858 Speech at Chicago

- "I have borne a laborious, and, in some respects to myself, a painful part in the contest. Through all, I have neither assailed, nor wrestled with any part of the constitution." -- October 30, 1858 Speech at Springfield

- "The people -- the people -- are the rightful masters of both congresses, and courts -- not to overthrow the constitution, but to overthrow the men who pervert it." -- September 16 and 17, 1859 Notes for Speeches at Columbus and Cincinnati

However, he had also proven to support concepts

that were not authorized by the Constitution:

- "I presume you all know who I am, I am humble Abraham Lincoln. I have been solicited by many friends to become a candidate for the legislature. My politics are short and sweet, like the old woman's dance. I am in favor of a national bank...in favor of the internal improvements system and a high protective tariff." – Abraham Lincoln, 1832[11]

The "national bank" he was referring to was Alexander Hamilton's creation, and the "internal improvements system" he supported was a clone of what President James Madison had vetoed in 1817 as being unconstitutional because he found no authority in the Constitution authorizing the federal government to take over the funding of internal improvements from the States.[12]

Later in his political career, Lincoln learned to use his words a little more wisely, concealing his true intentions while wrapping himself in the language of the Founding Fathers.

In the words of Abraham Lincoln's Gettysburg Address, he referred to the Declaration of Independence, asking if the United States as "a nation, conceived in liberty and dedicated to the proposition that all men are created equal...can long endure." The question, however, was what he meant as equality. Was Lincoln referring to the equality meant by Jefferson, which was created by God, and therefore places us as equals in His eyes, and the Blessings of Liberty and Natural Rights? Or was he referring to the kind of equality that exists "in the human heart [with] a depraved taste for equality, which impels the weak to attempt to lower the powerful to their own level, and reduces men to prefer equality in slavery to inequality in freedom?"[13]

During his presidency, Abraham Lincoln twisted the U.S. Constitution at will. He expanded the scope and power of the executive branch so that he could force upon the situation his will for the purpose of preserving the Union by coercing the rebel States into compliance under a powerful and supreme federal government.

Writer Frank J. Williams recognized and championed Lincoln's willingness to bend and twist the Constitution so that he could achieve his will, writing, "What made Lincoln a successful commander in chief was his constitutional flexibility, which allowed him to bend the Constitution within the framework of its intent without breaking it. Lincoln the lawyer-president avoided narrow overemphasis and understood the difference between distortion for personal aggrandizement and clarification for a higher purpose – that of preserving the greatest legal framework ever devised, the Constitution. Lincoln alternately preached to the American people and ordered arms to fulfill the true destiny of the Union as 'the last best hope of earth.' He could not have done this if he had not been first a lawyer [who was taught Marshall's legal philosophies] and then a president. Rather than limit himself to the role of commander in chief or attorney in chief, he used his background to deliver the greatest performance in his life in the courtroom of world opinion."[14]

Hence, the reason behind the importance of transitioning the United States into a democracy by silencing the voice of States' Rights by those who are unfaithful to the principles of the U.S. Constitution. In a democracy, if the statists can convince the voting public that tyranny is constitutional, and reinforce it with judicial opinion, then the people will gladly place the shackles of bondage upon their own ankles, themselves.

During his "benevolent dictatorship," Lincoln suspended constitutional liberties. He "suspended habeas corpus…ordered the arrest and imprisonment of virtually anyone who disagreed with his views – views that were new, radical, and not yet subject to any debate by the people's representatives in Congress or by the judiciary. In retrospect, no man who had the least bit of respect for constitutional liberty could ever have done such things. It would have been simply unthinkable to Jefferson, Madison, or Washington."[15]

"Lincoln rationalized this suspension of

constitutional liberties – at least in his own mind – with the rhetorical tool of falsely equating the Constitution with the Union. But the Constitution makes no mention of any 'perpetual' union, and one of the most distinguished constitutional scholars of the first half of the nineteenth century, William Rawle, forcefully argued that the Constitution contained an implicit recognition of the right of secession. That was certainly the belief of most Americans at the time. In the end, it was Lincoln's willingness to use brute military force, not his legal reasoning or his rhetorical talents, that allowed him to get away with such a radical assault on constitutional liberties."[16]

During his presidency, Lincoln suspended habeas corpus, suppressed free elections, initiated a suppression of the press, dissolved the Representative Houses repeatedly, imposed military rule on the parts of the South that became conquered territory, made judges dependent upon his will alone, erected a multitude of new offices with authorities outside those granted by the Constitution, quartered large bodies of troops among the citizens, imposed direct taxation without the consent of the governed, in many cases deprived persons of their right to a trial by jury, and he ordered the deportation of a political opponent (Congressman Clement L. Vallandigham, May 4, 1863).[17]

Lincoln's legacy, of which historians have paved over so that the truth may remain hidden, was an unnecessary war, the Reconstruction Period, and animosity among the races.

The dark hour of the War Between the States went against what had been intended by the Founding Fathers, and it interrupted an already ongoing peaceful move away from slavery in The South being orchestrated by a strong abolitionist movement, and the reality that slavery was simply no longer economically viable.

The cotton gin was the first piece of the puzzle leading to the demise of slavery in the United States. While its invention did not lessen the need for slaves during its early years, and in truth more slaves were needed in the field to keep up with the new machine, the invention of the cotton gin initiated an innovation revolution that led to other inventions that made producing cotton, and manufacturing cotton products, more efficient, moving the industry from the fields to the factory. In the long run, the emergence of new machinery was a key component in what would have ended slavery if there had not been an American Civil War. If war had never broken out, within a decade or two slavery would have been abolished State by State. In short, Lincoln's War Between the States unnecessarily slaughtered nearly 700,000 lives because using federal supremacy to force The South into compliance was more important to the Statists in power at the time than allowing the States to constitutionally abolish slavery on their own, individually.

The Reconstruction agenda that followed the war vastly expanded central state activity and expenditures, imposing a military occupation of The South, and employing a blatant disregard for constitutional liberties. The federal government did not totally succeed in centralizing all power in Washington, after the war, thanks to continued Southern political resistance, and a still-vibrant support among the American people for constitutionally limited government, but the federal government is vastly larger than the founders ever envisioned largely as a result of the War Between the States, and the subsequent Reconstruction Period.

In the movie "National Treasure," Nicolas Cage's character, Ben Gates, comments at one point in the movie, "Before the Civil War, the States were all separate. People used to say 'the United States are...' It wasn't until the war ended that people started saying 'the United States is...' Under Lincoln, we became one nation."

That was the whole point of Lincoln's war effort. While slavery was an ingredient, and he claimed to be in favor of freeing the slaves, the real goal was to change the United States from a federated union of States to a nation with silent States who are obedient to the powerful and supreme federal government.

While the debate may rage on for eternity regarding

whether or not Lincoln was a knowledgeable and willing participant in killing constitutionally mandated principles of State Sovereignty and States' Rights, the reality is that history has shown that the War Between the States, and the presidency of Abraham Lincoln, was the moment the concept of States' Rights began its final death spiral, and the moment that federal supremacy was finally able to grab both reins of the nation and drive her towards a fundamental change that would nearly be achieved during the dawn of the twenty-first century.

The most costly result of Lincoln's War Between the States is that the States not only lost their sovereignty, but in the process, like We the People during the twentieth century, the States become mere subjects to the federal government.

• Terms To Be Familiar With

Capitalism - An economic system characterized by private or corporate ownership of capital goods, by investments that are determined by private decision, and by prices, production, and the distribution of goods that are determined mainly by competition in a free market.

Central Government - A nationalistic government establishment; a governmental system that is typically a characteristic of a unitary state.

Communism - Socialism realized; theory of social organization based on principles of common ownership, ownership and possessions being ascribed to the community as a whole, or to the state. System in which all economic and social activity is controlled by a dominant government, administered by the ruling elite of a single, and self-perpetuating, political party.

Communitarianism - A society where the good of the community outweighs the good of the individual; a common good conception of justice; a well ordered society without rulers that uses pluralism as the guiding principle.

Congress - A legislative body granted the authority of legislative powers. In the United States, the Congress is the only part of government granted the authority of legislative powers.

Congress of the United States - The legislative branch of the federal government which consists of two houses, the Senate and House of Representatives. The Congress is the only part of the federal government granted the authority of legislative powers.

Constitutional Amendment - Changes made to an existing constitution.

Constitutional Republic - Government that adheres to the rule or authority of the principles of a constitution. A representative government that operates under the rule of law.

Council on Foreign Relations - United States nonprofit think tank specializing in U.S. foreign policy and international affairs. Membership is primarily reserved to influential politicians, academics, and media personalities; numbering in the thousands. The organization is believed to be a major player in the drive for a "New World Order" of internationalism, and the consolidation of power for globalists who are positioned as political and corporate elite. Pat Robertson in his book "The New World Order," suggested that the CFR was created because internationalists "realized America would not join any scheme for world government without a change in public opinion." The CFR has promoted the New World Order, controlled by the United Nations, and Pat Robertson suggests that the present United Nations organization is actually a creation of the CFR; Alger Hiss was the first Secretary-General and is often credited with the creation of the United Nations. Hiss was later discovered to be a Soviet spy.

Democracy - A form of government in which all citizens have an equal say in the decisions that affect their lives. Such a system includes equal participation in the proposal, development and passage of legislation into law.

Direct Taxation - A government levy on the income, property, or wealth of people or companies. A direct tax is borne entirely by the entity that pays it, and cannot be passed on to another entity.

Discretionary Spending - Government expenditures set on an annual basis, which can be adjusted year to year. Examples include defense budget, education, housing, transportation, and foreign aid.

Enumerated - Counted or told, number by number; reckoned or mentioned by distinct particulars.

Executive Order - An order issued by the President of the United States that may be a proclamation, or an order to change the processes within the Executive Branch.

Express Powers - Powers granted to the federal government by enumerated authorities expressly granted in the United States Constitution.

Fabianism - A type of socialism which emerged in Britain in 1884. Fabianism sought to use pure democracy as a bridge to establish a gradual conversion to socialism.

Fascism - A governmental system that regiments all industry and commerce through heavy regulatory controls. Characteristics of fascism often include the forced suppression of all opposition and criticism, aggressive nationalism, class warfare, and racial division.

Federal Government - System of government in which power is distributed between central authority and constituent territorial units.

Federal Reserve - A privately owned corporation owned by a secret group of international bankers. The Federal Reserve holds a monopoly on the creation of money in the United States. Whenever the U.S. Government needs money it borrows the money from the federal reserve, thus creating a national debt.

Federalism - Government in which the central

government's power and authority is limited by local government units, and where each unit is delegated a sphere of power and authority only it can exercise, while other powers must be shared. The term federalism comes from the Latin root *foedus*, which means "formal agreement or covenant." It includes the interrelationships between the states as well as between the states and the federal government.

Federalist Papers - The Federalist [Papers] are a collection of 85 articles and essays written in late 1787 and the first half of 1788 under the pseudonym "Publius" (after the founder of the Roman Republic) by Alexander Hamilton (51), James Madison (29), and John Jay (5) to promote the ratification of the United States Constitution. The identities of the writers as the authors of the Federalist Papers remained unknown until after 1810 (about six years after Hamilton's death from a dual with Aaron Burr in 1804) based on a list left by Hamilton which associated the authors with their numbers. While the authorship had been a closely guarded secret, because from the British point of view the former colonists were committing treason against the British Empire (Great Britain refused to recognize the sovereignty of the United States, and view the States as anything different than British Colonies, until after the War of 1812), astute observers discerned the identities as Hamilton, Madison, and Jay as the essays were being released. However, it wasn't until 1944 that Douglass Adair postulated the assignments of authorship, which was corroborated in 1964 by a computer analysis of the text. The Federalist articles appeared in three New York newspapers: The Independent Journal, the New-York Packet, and the Daily Advertiser, beginning on October 27, 1787. Most of them begin with the same salutation: "To the People of the State of New York". On January 1, 1788, the New York publishing firm J. & A. McLean announced that they would publish the first thirty-six essays as a bound volume which was released on March 2 and was titled *The Federalist*. New essays continued to appear in the newspapers. A second bound volume containing the last forty-nine essays was released on May 28. The remaining eight were published in the New York newspapers between June 14 and August 16.

Foreign Entanglements - Unnecessary involvement with other nations.

Free Market - Market economy in which the exchange of goods and services, and the fluctuation of prices, are free from intervention by government; an economic system governed by competition among private businesses, and the forces of supply and demand.

General Will – A political theory based on the concept that the true will of the people is not always recognized by the general public, so in order to ensure the public good a ruling elite capable of comprehending the general will must interpret and apply the general will for the common good. To avoid tyranny, the ruling elite must be trusted to serve the general will, not their own individual interests.

Ideology - A set of political or economic ideas that forms the basis of economic or political theory and policy.

Implied Authority - Concept granting to an agent with implied jurisdiction the authority to perform acts considered reasonably necessary to accomplish the purpose of an overall organization or body. Under contract law, implied authority figures have the ability to make a legally binding contract on behalf of another person or company.

Jacobinism - An ideology that emerged from a radical society that existed prior, and during, the French Revolution and the subsequent Reign of Terror. The club was comprised of wealthy members of French Society who claimed to stand in the camp of the working class so as to maintain their power base. While the Jacobins became the dominant power in revolutionary France for several years, their oligarchy was ultimately replaced by a succession of more totalitarian regimes. In today's vernacular, Jacobin is typically associated with the concept of an extreme radical willing to kill his opponents to accomplish his aims. Considered leftwing in French Society, and on today's American Political Spectrum.

Judicial Activism - When judges violate the Separation of Powers through their rulings; when a judge rules legislatively by modifying or striking down a law using the unconstitutional authority of judicial review.

Judicial Branch - The branch of the United States Government responsible for the administration of justice; a central judiciary that is limited to federal authorities, and separated from the will of the central leadership.

Judicial Review - The unconstitutional authority of the federal courts to review law, interpret the Constitution regarding laws, and then determine the constitutionality of laws.

Laissez Faire - A policy or attitude of letting things take their own course, without interfering. Abstention by governments from interfering in the workings of the free market.

Limited Government - A government that acts within the limitations granted to it; a governmental system that is restrained by an enumerated list of authorities; a limited government is the essence of liberty.

Maladministration - Inefficient or dishonest administration; mismanagement.

Mandatory Spending - Government spending

automatically obligated due to previously enacted laws. Examples include benefits programs, entitlements, Social Security.

Marxism - A revolutionary movement developed by the German scholar and activist Karl Marx and his collaborator Friedrich Engels. The premise of Marxism is that society exists through class struggles. The goal is to establish a classless society by displacing capitalism, and other non-socialist constructs. In theory, Marx's socialism, after a transitional period of revolutionary dictatorship, will fade away to be replaced by communism – a culture of collective ownership and societal cooperation.

Mercantilism - The use of protectionism to control trade and commerce, while generating wealth for a government through the accumulation of profitable balances.

Nationalism - Political ideology which involves a strong identification of a group of individuals with a political entity defined in national terms. There are various strands of nationalism. The ideology may dictate that citizenship in a state should be limited to one ethnic, cultural or identity group. Nationalism may also include the belief that the state is of primary importance, which becomes the unhealthy love of one's government, accompanied by the aggressive desire to build that governmental system to a point that it is above all else, and becomes the ultimate provider for the public good.

Nationalist - An advocate of Nationalism.

Oligarchy - Government by a few powerful persons, over the many. A state governed by a few persons.

Original Intent - Original meaning of the United States Constitution as intended by the framers during the Federal Convention of 1787, and the subsequent State Ratification Conventions.

Originalist view of the Constitution - View that the Constitution as written should be interpreted in a manner consistent with what was meant by those who drafted and ratified it.

Political Spectrum - A broad range of political philosophies; the level of control of government over a society.

Progressive Era - Period spanning from about 1890 to 1920 noted for a steady stream of political reforms, an attempt at the purifying of society from social ills, and promoting efficiency through an increase in federal programs. While socialists did not favor the progressive movement early on because it sought to strengthen capitalism, the Democrats favored the era because it pushed to enable the citizenry to rule more directly. Primary Elections were also introduced during the Progressive Era, as were the 16th and 17th Amendments (income tax and changing the U.S. Senate from appointment to democratically elected), and the Federal Reserve.

Progressivism - Philosophy that views progress as seeking change in approaches to solving economic, social, and other problems, often through government sponsored programs.

Quorum: Minimum number required in order to conduct business.

Redistribution of Wealth - Transfer of income and wealth from some individuals to others through governmental mechanisms such as taxation, regulations, and bureaucracy, and through social schemes, reforms, policies or confiscatory actions.

Rule of Law - The restriction of the arbitrary exercise of power by subordinating it to well-defined and established laws; Laws of Nature and of Nature's God; self-evident standard of conduct and law.

Rule of Man - The unrestricted exercise of power by a ruling elite who adjust the law based on the whims of society, or the interpretation of the law by ruling class, or judicial class; a living breathing system of law.

Social Contract - An implicit agreement among the members of a society to cooperate for social benefits.

Socialism - An economic system in which goods and

services are provided through a central system of cooperative and/or government ownership rather than through competition and a free market system.

State Sovereignty - The individual autonomy of the several states; strong local government was considered the key to freedom; a limited government is the essence of liberty.

States' Rights - The authorities of the States over local issues, and other issues, that are not directly related to the preservation of the union or are considered as federal issues.

Statism - A system in which the concentration of economic controls and planning are consolidated in the hands of a highly centralized government. These controls, in a system of statism, often extend to government ownership, or heavy regulation by the government, of private industry.

Statist - An advocate of statism, which is a system in which the concentration of economic controls and planning in the hands of a highly centralized government often extend to government ownership of industry.

Statists - Individuals who hold that government should control the economic and social policies of the system it serves.

Tyranny - Arbitrary, or despotic, exercise of power;

the exercise of power over subjects and others with a rigor not authorized by law or justice, or not requisite for the purposes of government. Hence tyranny is often synonymous with cruelty and oppression; a cruel government.

• United States Constitution

Changed or obsolete passages are in [brackets]

Preamble

We the People of the United States, in Order to form a more perfect Union, establish Justice, insure domestic Tranquility, provide for the common defence, promote the general Welfare, and secure the Blessings of Liberty to ourselves and our Posterity, do ordain and establish this Constitution for the United States of America.

Article I

Section 1

All legislative Powers herein granted shall be vested in a Congress of the United States, which shall consist of a Senate and House of Representatives.

Section 2

The House of Representatives shall be composed of Members chosen every second Year by the People of the several States, and the Electors in each State shall have the Qualifications requisite for Electors of the most numerous Branch of the State Legislature.

No Person shall be a Representative who shall not have attained to the Age of twenty five Years, and been seven Years a Citizen of the United States, and who shall not, when elected, be an Inhabitant of that State in which he shall be chosen.

[Representatives and direct Taxes shall be apportioned among the several States which may be included within this Union, according to their respective Numbers, which shall be determined by adding to the whole Number of free Persons, including those bound to Service for a Term of Years, and excluding Indians not taxed, three fifths of all other Persons.] *(Changed by section 2 of the Fourteenth Amendment)* The actual Enumeration shall be made within three Years after the first Meeting of the Congress of the United States, and within every subsequent Term of ten Years, in such Manner as they shall by Law direct. The Number of Representatives shall not exceed one for every thirty Thousand, but each State shall have at Least one Representative; and until such enumeration shall be made, the State of New Hampshire shall be entitled to chuse three, Massachusetts eight, Rhode-Island and Providence Plantations one, Connecticut five, New-York six, New Jersey four, Pennsylvania eight, Delaware one, Maryland six, Virginia ten, North Carolina five, South Carolina five, and Georgia three.

When vacancies happen in the Representation from any State, the Executive Authority thereof shall issue Writs of Election to fill such Vacancies.

The House of Representatives shall chuse their Speaker and other Officers; and shall have the sole Power of Impeachment.

Section 3

The Senate of the United States shall be composed of two Senators from each State, [chosen by the Legislature thereof] *(Changed by the Seventeenth Amendment)* for six Years; and each Senator shall have one Vote.

Immediately after they shall be assembled in Consequence of the first Election, they shall be divided as equally as may be into three Classes. The Seats of the Senators of the first Class shall be vacated at the Expiration of the second Year, of the second Class at the Expiration of the fourth Year, and of the third Class at the Expiration of the sixth Year, so that one third may be chosen every second Year; [and if Vacancies happen by Resignation, or otherwise, during the Recess of the Legislature of any State, the Executive thereof may make temporary Appointments until the next Meeting of the Legislature, which shall then fill such Vacancies.] *(Changed by the Seventeenth Amendment)*

No Person shall be a Senator who shall not have attained to the Age of thirty Years, and been nine Years a Citizen of the United States, and who shall not, when elected, be an Inhabitant of that State for which he shall be chosen.

The Vice President of the United States shall be President of the Senate, but shall have no Vote, unless they be equally divided.

The Senate shall chuse their other Officers, and also a President pro tempore, in the Absence of the Vice President, or when he shall exercise the Office of President of the United States.

The Senate shall have the sole Power to try all Impeachments. When sitting for that Purpose, they shall be on Oath or Affirmation. When the President of the United States is tried, the Chief Justice shall preside: And no Person shall be convicted without the Concurrence of two thirds of the Members present.

Judgment in Cases of Impeachment shall not extend further than to removal from Office, and disqualification to hold and enjoy any Office of honor, Trust or Profit under the United States: but the Party convicted shall nevertheless be liable and subject to Indictment, Trial, Judgment and Punishment, according to Law.

Section 4

The Times, Places and Manner of holding Elections for Senators and Representatives, shall be prescribed in each State by the Legislature thereof; but the

Congress may at any time by Law make or alter such Regulations, except as to the Places of chusing Senators.

The Congress shall assemble at least once in every Year, and such Meeting shall be [on the first Monday in December,] *(Changed by Section 2 of the Twentieth Amendment)* unless they shall by Law appoint a different Day.

Section 5

Each House shall be the Judge of the Elections, Returns and Qualifications of its own Members, and a Majority of each shall constitute a Quorum to do Business; but a smaller Number may adjourn from day to day, and may be authorized to compel the Attendance of absent Members, in such Manner, and under such Penalties as each House may provide.

Each House may determine the Rules of its Proceedings, punish its Members for disorderly Behaviour, and, with the Concurrence of two thirds, expel a Member.

Each House shall keep a Journal of its Proceedings, and from time to time publish the same, excepting such Parts as may in their Judgment require Secrecy; and the Yeas and Nays of the Members of either House on any question shall, at the Desire of one fifth of those Present, be entered on the Journal.

Neither House, during the Session of Congress, shall, without the Consent of the other, adjourn for more than three days, nor to any other Place than that in which the two Houses shall be sitting.

Section 6

The Senators and Representatives shall receive a Compensation for their Services, to be ascertained by Law, and paid out of the Treasury of the United States. They shall in all Cases, except Treason, Felony and Breach of the Peace, be privileged from Arrest during their Attendance at the Session of their respective Houses, and in going to and returning from the same; and for any Speech or Debate in either House, they shall not be questioned in any other Place.

No Senator or Representative shall, during the Time for which he was elected, be appointed to any civil Office under the Authority of the United States, which shall have been created, or the Emoluments whereof shall have been encreased during such time; and no Person holding any Office under the United States, shall be a Member of either House during his Continuance in Office.

Section 7

All Bills for raising Revenue shall originate in the House of Representatives; but the Senate may propose or concur with Amendments as on other

Bills.

Every Bill which shall have passed the House of Representatives and the Senate, shall, before it become a Law, be presented to the President of the United States: If he approve he shall sign it, but if not he shall return it, with his Objections to that House in which it shall have originated, who shall enter the Objections at large on their Journal, and proceed to reconsider it. If after such Reconsideration two thirds of that House shall agree to pass the Bill, it shall be sent, together with the Objections, to the other House, by which it shall likewise be reconsidered, and if approved by two thirds of that House, it shall become a Law. But in all such Cases the Votes of both Houses shall be determined by yeas and Nays, and the Names of the Persons voting for and against the Bill shall be entered on the Journal of each House respectively. If any Bill shall not be returned by the President within ten Days (Sundays excepted) after it shall have been presented to him, the Same shall be a Law, in like Manner as if he had signed it, unless the Congress by their Adjournment prevent its Return, in which Case it shall not be a Law.

Every Order, Resolution, or Vote to which the Concurrence of the Senate and House of Representatives may be necessary (except on a question of Adjournment) shall be presented to the President of the United States; and before the Same shall take Effect, shall be approved by him, or being disapproved by him, shall be repassed by two thirds of the Senate and House of Representatives, according to the Rules and Limitations prescribed in the Case of a Bill.

Section 8

The Congress shall have Power To lay and collect Taxes, Duties, Imposts and Excises, to pay the Debts and provide for the common Defence and general Welfare of the United States; but all Duties, Imposts and Excises shall be uniform throughout the United States;

To borrow Money on the credit of the United States;

To regulate Commerce with foreign Nations, and among the several States, and with the Indian Tribes;

To establish an uniform Rule of Naturalization, and uniform Laws on the subject of Bankruptcies throughout the United States;

To coin Money, regulate the Value thereof, and of foreign Coin, and fix the Standard of Weights and Measures;

To provide for the Punishment of counterfeiting the Securities and current Coin of the United States;

To establish Post Offices and post Roads;

To promote the Progress of Science and useful Arts, by securing for limited Times to Authors and Inventors the exclusive Right to their respective Writings and Discoveries;

To constitute Tribunals inferior to the supreme Court;

To define and punish Piracies and Felonies committed on the high Seas, and Offences against the Law of Nations;

To declare War, grant Letters of Marque and Reprisal, and make Rules concerning Captures on Land and Water;

To raise and support Armies, but no Appropriation of Money to that Use shall be for a longer Term than two Years;

To provide and maintain a Navy;

To make Rules for the Government and Regulation of the land and naval Forces;

To provide for calling forth the Militia to execute the Laws of the Union, suppress Insurrections and repel Invasions;

To provide for organizing, arming, and disciplining, the Militia, and for governing such Part of them as may be employed in the Service of the United States, reserving to the States respectively, the Appointment of the Officers, and the Authority of training the Militia according to the discipline prescribed by Congress;

To exercise exclusive Legislation in all Cases whatsoever, over such District (not exceeding ten Miles square) as may, by Cession of particular States, and the Acceptance of Congress, become the Seat of the Government of the United States, and to exercise like Authority over all Places purchased by the Consent of the Legislature of the State in which the Same shall be, for the Erection of Forts, Magazines, Arsenals, dock-Yards, and other needful Buildings;--And

To make all Laws which shall be necessary and proper for carrying into Execution the foregoing Powers, and all other Powers vested by this Constitution in the Government of the United States, or in any Department or Officer thereof.

Section 9

The Migration or Importation of such Persons as any of the States now existing shall think proper to admit, shall not be prohibited by the Congress prior to the Year one thousand eight hundred and eight, but a Tax or duty may be imposed on such Importation, not exceeding ten dollars for each Person.

The Privilege of the Writ of Habeas Corpus shall not be suspended, unless when in Cases of Rebellion or Invasion the public Safety may require it.

No Bill of Attainder or ex post facto Law shall be passed.

No Capitation, or other direct, Tax shall be laid, unless in Proportion to the Census or enumeration herein before directed to be taken.

No Tax or Duty shall be laid on Articles exported from any State.

No Preference shall be given by any Regulation of Commerce or Revenue to the Ports of one State over those of another; nor shall Vessels bound to, or from, one State, be obliged to enter, clear, or pay Duties in another.

No Money shall be drawn from the Treasury, but in Consequence of Appropriations made by Law; and a regular Statement and Account of the Receipts and Expenditures of all public Money shall be published from time to time.

No Title of Nobility shall be granted by the United States: And no Person holding any Office of Profit or Trust under them, shall, without the Consent of the Congress, accept of any present, Emolument, Office, or Title, of any kind whatever, from any King, Prince, or foreign State.

Section 10

No State shall enter into any Treaty, Alliance, or Confederation; grant Letters of Marque and Reprisal; coin Money; emit Bills of Credit; make any Thing but gold and silver Coin a Tender in Payment of Debts; pass any Bill of Attainder, ex post facto Law, or Law impairing the Obligation of Contracts, or grant any Title of Nobility.

No State shall, without the Consent of the Congress, lay any Imposts or Duties on Imports or Exports, except what may be absolutely necessary for executing it's inspection Laws: and the net Produce of all Duties and Imposts, laid by any State on Imports or Exports, shall be for the Use of the Treasury of the United States; and all such Laws shall be subject to the Revision and Controul of the Congress.

No State shall, without the Consent of Congress, lay any Duty of Tonnage, keep Troops, or Ships of War in time of Peace, enter into any Agreement or Compact with another State, or with a foreign Power, or engage in War, unless actually invaded, or in such imminent Danger as will not admit of delay.

Article II

Section 1

The executive Power shall be vested in a President of the United States of America. He shall hold his Office during the Term of four Years, and, together with the Vice President, chosen for the same Term, be elected, as follows:

Each State shall appoint, in such Manner as the Legislature thereof may direct, a Number of Electors, equal to the whole Number of Senators and Representatives to which the State may be entitled in the Congress: but no Senator or Representative, or Person holding an Office of Trust or Profit under the United States, shall be appointed an Elector.

[The Electors shall meet in their respective States, and vote by Ballot for two Persons, of whom one at least shall not be an Inhabitant of the same State with themselves. And they shall make a List of all the Persons voted for, and of the Number of Votes for each; which List they shall sign and certify, and transmit sealed to the Seat of the Government of the United States, directed to the President of the Senate. The President of the Senate shall, in the Presence of the Senate and House of Representatives, open all the Certificates, and the Votes shall then be counted. The Person having the greatest Number of Votes shall be the President, if such Number be a Majority of the whole Number of Electors appointed; and if there be more than one who have such Majority, and have an equal Number of Votes, then the House of Representatives shall immediately chuse by Ballot one of them for President; and if no Person have a

Majority, then from the five highest on the List the said House shall in like Manner chuse the President. But in chusing the President, the Votes shall be taken by States, the Representation from each State having one Vote; A quorum for this purpose shall consist of a Member or Members from two thirds of the States, and a Majority of all the States shall be necessary to a Choice. In every Case, after the Choice of the President, the Person having the greatest Number of Votes of the Electors shall be the Vice President. But if there should remain two or more who have equal Votes, the Senate shall chuse from them by Ballot the Vice President.] *(Changed by the Twelfth Amendment)*

The Congress may determine the Time of chusing the Electors, and the Day on which they shall give their Votes; which Day shall be the same throughout the United States.

No Person except a natural born Citizen, or a Citizen of the United States, at the time of the Adoption of this Constitution, shall be eligible to the Office of President; neither shall any Person be eligible to that Office who shall not have attained to the Age of thirty five Years, and been fourteen Years a Resident within the United States.

[In Case of the Removal of the President from Office, or of his Death, Resignation, or Inability to discharge the Powers and Duties of the said Office, the Same shall devolve on the Vice President, and the Congress may by Law provide for the Case of Removal, Death, Resignation or Inability, both of the President and Vice President, declaring what Officer shall then act as President, and such Officer shall act accordingly, until the Disability be removed, or a President shall be elected.] *(Changed by the Twenty-Fifth Amendment)*

The President shall, at stated Times, receive for his Services, a Compensation, which shall neither be increased nor diminished during the Period for which he shall have been elected, and he shall not receive within that Period any other Emolument from the United States, or any of them.

Before he enter on the Execution of his Office, he shall take the following Oath or Affirmation:--"I do solemnly swear (or affirm) that I will faithfully execute the Office of President of the United States, and will to the best of my Ability, preserve, protect and defend the Constitution of the United States."

Section 2

The President shall be Commander in Chief of the Army and Navy of the United States, and of the Militia of the several States, when called into the actual Service of the United States; he may require the Opinion, in writing, of the principal Officer in each of the executive Departments, upon any Subject relating to the Duties of their respective Offices, and he shall have Power to grant Reprieves and Pardons for Offences against the United States, except in Cases of Impeachment.

He shall have Power, by and with the Advice and Consent of the Senate, to make Treaties, provided two thirds of the Senators present concur; and he shall nominate, and by and with the Advice and Consent of the Senate, shall appoint Ambassadors, other public Ministers and Consuls, Judges of the supreme Court, and all other Officers of the United States, whose Appointments are not herein otherwise provided for, and which shall be established by Law: but the Congress may by Law vest the Appointment of such inferior Officers, as they think proper, in the President alone, in the Courts of Law, or in the Heads of Departments.

The President shall have Power to fill up all Vacancies that may happen during the Recess of the Senate, by granting Commissions which shall expire at the End of their next Session.

Section 3

He shall from time to time give to the Congress Information of the State of the Union, and recommend to their Consideration such Measures as he shall judge necessary and expedient; he may, on extraordinary Occasions, convene both Houses, or either of them, and in Case of Disagreement between them, with Respect to the Time of Adjournment, he may adjourn them to such Time as he shall think proper; he shall receive Ambassadors and other public Ministers; he shall take Care that the Laws be faithfully executed, and shall Commission all the Officers of the United States.

Section 4

The President, Vice President and all civil Officers of the United States, shall be removed from Office on Impeachment for, and Conviction of, Treason, **Bribery**, or other high Crimes and Misdemeanors.

Article III

Section 1

The judicial Power of the United States shall be vested in one supreme Court, and in such inferior Courts as the Congress may from time to time ordain and establish. The Judges, both of the supreme and inferior Courts, shall hold their Offices during good Behaviour, and shall, at stated Times, receive for their Services a Compensation, which shall not be diminished during their Continuance in Office.

Section 2

The judicial Power shall extend to all Cases, in Law and Equity, arising under this Constitution, the Laws of the United States, and Treaties made, or which shall be made, under their Authority;--to all Cases affecting Ambassadors, other public Ministers and

Consuls;--to all Cases of admiralty and maritime Jurisdiction;--to Controversies to which the United States shall be a Party;--to Controversies between two or more States;-- [between a State and Citizens of another State,] *(Changed by the Eleventh Amendment)* --between Citizens of different States,-- between Citizens of the same State claiming Lands under Grants of different States, [and between a State, or the Citizens thereof, and foreign States, Citizens or Subjects.] *(Changed by the Eleventh Amendment)*

In all Cases affecting Ambassadors, other public Ministers and Consuls, and those in which a State shall be Party, the supreme Court shall have original Jurisdiction. In all the other Cases before mentioned, the supreme Court shall have appellate Jurisdiction, both as to Law and Fact, with such Exceptions, and under such Regulations as the Congress shall make.

The Trial of all Crimes, except in Cases of Impeachment, shall be by Jury; and such Trial shall be held in the State where the said Crimes shall have been committed; but when not committed within any State, the Trial shall be at such Place or Places as the Congress may by Law have directed.

Section 3

Treason against the United States, shall consist only in levying War against them, or in adhering to their Enemies, giving them Aid and Comfort. No Person shall be convicted of Treason unless on the Testimony of two Witnesses to the same overt Act, or on Confession in open Court.

The Congress shall have Power to declare the Punishment of Treason, but no Attainder of Treason shall work Corruption of Blood, or Forfeiture except during the Life of the Person attainted.

Article IV

Section 1

Full Faith and Credit shall be given in each State to the public Acts, Records, and judicial Proceedings of every other State. And the Congress may by general Laws prescribe the Manner in which such Acts, Records and Proceedings shall be proved, and the Effect thereof.

Section 2

The Citizens of each State shall be entitled to all Privileges and Immunities of Citizens in the several States.

A Person charged in any State with Treason, Felony, or other Crime, who shall flee from Justice, and be found in another State, shall on Demand of the executive Authority of the State from which he fled, be delivered up, to be removed to the State having Jurisdiction of the Crime.

[No Person held to Service or Labour in one State, under the Laws thereof, escaping into another, shall, in Consequence of any Law or Regulation therein, be discharged from such Service or Labour, but shall be delivered up on Claim of the Party to whom such Service or Labour may be due.] *(Changed by the Thirteenth Amendment)*

Section 3

New States may be admitted by the Congress into this Union; but no new State shall be formed or erected within the Jurisdiction of any other State; nor any State be formed by the Junction of two or more States, or Parts of States, without the Consent of the Legislatures of the States concerned as well as of the Congress.

The Congress shall have Power to dispose of and make all needful Rules and Regulations respecting the Territory or other Property belonging to the United States; and nothing in this Constitution shall be so construed as to Prejudice any Claims of the United States, or of any particular State.

Section 4

The United States shall guarantee to every State in this Union a Republican Form of Government, and shall protect each of them against Invasion; and on Application of the Legislature, or of the Executive (when the Legislature cannot be convened), against domestic Violence.

Article V

The Congress, whenever two thirds of both Houses shall deem it necessary, shall propose Amendments to this Constitution, or, on the Application of the Legislatures of two thirds of the several States, shall call a Convention for proposing Amendments, which, in either Case, shall be valid to all Intents and Purposes, as Part of this Constitution, when ratified by the Legislatures of three fourths of the several States, or by Conventions in three fourths thereof, as the one or the other Mode of Ratification may be proposed by the Congress; Provided that no Amendment which may be made prior to the Year One thousand eight hundred and eight shall in any Manner affect the first and fourth Clauses in the Ninth Section of the first Article; and that no State, without its Consent, shall be deprived of its equal Suffrage in the Senate.

Article VI

All Debts contracted and Engagements entered into, before the Adoption of this Constitution, shall be as valid against the United States under this Constitution, as under the Confederation.

This Constitution, and the Laws of the United States which shall be made in Pursuance thereof; and all

Treaties made, or which shall be made, under the Authority of the United States, shall be the supreme Law of the Land; and the Judges in every State shall be bound thereby, any Thing in the Constitution or Laws of any State to the Contrary notwithstanding.

The Senators and Representatives before mentioned, and the Members of the several State Legislatures, and all executive and judicial Officers, both of the United States and of the several States, shall be bound by Oath or Affirmation, to support this Constitution; but no religious Test shall ever be required as a Qualification to any Office or public Trust under the United States.

Article VII

The Ratification of the Conventions of nine States, shall be sufficient for the Establishment of this Constitution between the States so ratifying the Same.

done in Convention by the Unanimous Consent of the States present the Seventeenth Day of September in the Year of our Lord one thousand seven hundred and Eighty seven and of the Independance of the United States of America the Twelfth In witness whereof We have hereunto subscribed our Names,

G°. Washington
Presidt and deputy from Virginia

Delaware
Geo: Read
Gunning Bedford jun
John Dickinson
Richard Bassett
Jaco: Broom

Maryland
James McHenry
Dan of St Thos. Jenifer
Danl. Carroll

Virginia
John Blair
James Madison Jr.

North Carolina
Wm. Blount
Richd. Dobbs Spaight
Hu Williamson

South Carolina
J. Rutledge
Charles Cotesworth Pinckney
Charles Pinckney
Pierce Butler

Georgia
William Few
Abr Baldwin

New Hampshire

John Langdon
Nicholas Gilman

Massachusetts
Nathaniel Gorham
Rufus King

Connecticut
Wm. Saml. Johnson
Roger Sherman

New York
Alexander Hamilton

New Jersey
Wil: Livingston
David Brearley
Wm. Paterson
Jona: Dayton

Pennsylvania
B Franklin
Thomas Mifflin
Robt. Morris
Geo. Clymer
Thos. FitzSimons
Jared Ingersoll
James Wilson
Gouv Morris

Bill of Rights – Amendments 1-10, Ratified December 15, 1791

Amendment I

Congress shall make no law respecting an establishment of religion, or prohibiting the free exercise thereof; or abridging the freedom of speech, or of the press; or the right of the people peaceably to assemble, and to petition the Government for a redress of grievances.

Amendment II

A well regulated Militia, being necessary to the security of a free State, the right of the people to keep and bear Arms, shall not be infringed.

Amendment III

No Soldier shall, in time of peace be quartered in any house, without the consent of the Owner, nor in time of war, but in a manner to be prescribed by law.

Amendment IV

The right of the people to be secure in their persons, houses, papers, and effects, against unreasonable searches and seizures, shall not be violated, and no Warrants shall issue, but upon probable cause, supported by Oath or affirmation, and particularly describing the place to be searched, and the persons or things to be seized.

Amendment V

No person shall be held to answer for a capital, or otherwise infamous crime, unless on a presentment or indictment of a Grand Jury, except in cases arising in the land or naval forces, or in the Militia, when in actual service in time of War or public danger; nor shall any person be subject for the same offence to be twice put in jeopardy of life or limb; nor shall be compelled in any criminal case to be a witness against himself, nor be deprived of life, liberty, or property, without due process of law; nor shall private property be taken for public use, without just compensation.

Amendment VI

In all criminal prosecutions, the accused shall enjoy the right to a speedy and public trial, by an impartial jury of the State and district wherein the crime shall have been committed, which district shall have been previously ascertained by law, and to be informed of the nature and cause of the accusation; to be confronted with the witnesses against him; to have compulsory process for obtaining witnesses in his favor, and to have the Assistance of Counsel for his defence.

Amendment VII

In Suits at common law, where the value in controversy shall exceed twenty dollars, the right of trial by jury shall be preserved, and no fact tried by a jury, shall be otherwise re-examined in any Court of the United States, than according to the rules of the common law.

Amendment VIII

Excessive bail shall not be required, nor excessive fines imposed, nor cruel and unusual punishments inflicted.

Amendment IX

The enumeration in the Constitution, of certain rights, shall not be construed to deny or disparage others retained by the people.

Amendment X

The powers not delegated to the United States by the Constitution, nor prohibited by it to the States, are reserved to the States respectively, or to the people.

Amendments 11-27

Amendment XI

Passed by Congress March 4, 1794. Ratified

February 7, 1795.

The Judicial power of the United States shall not be construed to extend to any suit in law or equity, commenced or prosecuted against one of the United States by Citizens of another State, or by Citizens or Subjects of any Foreign State.

Amendment XII

Passed by Congress December 9, 1803. Ratified June 15, 1804.

The Electors shall meet in their respective states and vote by ballot for President and Vice-President, one of whom, at least, shall not be an inhabitant of the same state with themselves; they shall name in their ballots the person voted for as President, and in distinct ballots the person voted for as Vice-President, and they shall make distinct lists of all persons voted for as President, and of all persons voted for as Vice-President, and of the number of votes for each, which lists they shall sign and certify, and transmit sealed to the seat of the government of the United States, directed to the President of the Senate; -- the President of the Senate shall, in the presence of the Senate and House of Representatives, open all the certificates and the votes shall then be counted; -- The person having the greatest number of votes for President, shall be the President, if such number be a majority of the whole number of Electors appointed; and if no person have such majority, then from the persons having the highest numbers not exceeding three on the list of those voted for as President, the House of Representatives shall choose immediately, by ballot, the President. But in choosing the President, the votes shall be taken by states, the representation from each state having one vote; a quorum for this purpose shall consist of a member or members from two-thirds of the states, and a majority of all the states shall be necessary to a choice. [And if the House of Representatives shall not choose a President whenever the right of choice shall devolve upon them, before the fourth day of March next following, then the Vice-President shall act as President, as in case of the death or other constitutional disability of the President.] *(Superseded by section 3 of the Twentieth Amendment)* The person having the greatest number of votes as Vice-President, shall be the Vice-President, if such number be a majority of the whole number of Electors appointed, and if no person have a majority, then from the two highest numbers on the list, the Senate shall choose the Vice-President; a quorum for the purpose shall consist of two-thirds of the whole number of Senators, and a majority of the whole number shall be necessary to a choice. But no person constitutionally ineligible to the office of President shall be eligible to that of Vice-President of the United States.

Amendment XIII

Passed by Congress January 31, 1865. Ratified December 6, 1865.

Section 1.
Neither slavery nor involuntary servitude, except as a punishment for crime whereof the party shall have been duly convicted, shall exist within the United States, or any place subject to their jurisdiction.

Section 2.
Congress shall have power to enforce this article by appropriate legislation.

Amendment XIV

Passed by Congress June 13, 1866. Ratified July 9, 1868.

Section 1.
All persons born or naturalized in the United States, and subject to the jurisdiction thereof, are citizens of the United States and of the State wherein they reside. No State shall make or enforce any law which shall abridge the privileges or immunities of citizens of the United States; nor shall any State deprive any person of life, liberty, or property, without due process of law; nor deny to any person within its jurisdiction the equal protection of the laws.

Section 2.

Representatives shall be apportioned among the several States according to their respective numbers, counting the whole number of persons in each State, excluding Indians not taxed. But when the right to vote at any election for the choice of electors for President and Vice-President of the United States, Representatives in Congress, the Executive and Judicial officers of a State, or the members of the Legislature thereof, is denied to any of the male inhabitants of such State, [being twenty-one years of age,] *(Changed by section 1 of the 26th amendment)* and citizens of the United States, or in any way abridged, except for participation in rebellion, or other crime, the basis of representation therein shall be reduced in the proportion which the number of such male citizens shall bear to the whole number of male citizens twenty-one years of age in such State.

Section 3.
No person shall be a Senator or Representative in Congress, or elector of President and Vice-President, or hold any office, civil or military, under the United States, or under any State, who, having previously taken an oath, as a member of Congress, or as an officer of the United States, or as a member of any State legislature, or as an executive or judicial officer of any State, to support the Constitution of the United States, shall have engaged in insurrection or rebellion against the same, or given aid or comfort to the enemies thereof. But Congress may by a vote of two-thirds of each House, remove such disability.

Section 4.

The validity of the public debt of the United States, authorized by law, including debts incurred for payment of pensions and bounties for services in suppressing insurrection or rebellion, shall not be questioned. But neither the United States nor any State shall assume or pay any debt or obligation incurred in aid of insurrection or rebellion against the United States, or any claim for the loss or emancipation of any slave; but all such debts, obligations and claims shall be held illegal and void.

Section 5.

The Congress shall have the power to enforce, by appropriate legislation, the provisions of this article.

Amendment XV

Passed by Congress February 26, 1869. Ratified February 3, 1870.

Section 1.

The right of citizens of the United States to vote shall not be denied or abridged by the United States or by any State on account of race, color, or previous condition of servitude--

Section 2.

The Congress shall have the power to enforce this article by appropriate legislation.

Amendment XVI

Passed by Congress July 2, 1909. Ratified February 3, 1913.

The Congress shall have power to lay and collect taxes on incomes, from whatever source derived, without apportionment among the several States, and without regard to any census or enumeration.

Amendment XVII

Passed by Congress May 13, 1912. Ratified April 8, 1913.

The Senate of the United States shall be composed of two Senators from each State, elected by the people thereof, for six years; and each Senator shall have one vote. The electors in each State shall have the qualifications requisite for electors of the most numerous branch of the State legislatures.

When vacancies happen in the representation of any State in the Senate, the executive authority of such State shall issue writs of election to fill such vacancies: Provided, That the legislature of any State may empower the executive thereof to make temporary appointments until the people fill the vacancies by election as the legislature may direct.

This amendment shall not be so construed as to affect the election or term of any Senator chosen before it becomes valid as part of the Constitution.

Amendment XVIII

Passed by Congress December 18, 1917. Ratified January 16, 1919.

[Section 1.
After one year from the ratification of this article the manufacture, sale, or transportation of intoxicating liquors within, the importation thereof into, or the exportation thereof from the United States and all territory subject to the jurisdiction thereof for beverage purposes is hereby prohibited.

Section 2.
The Congress and the several States shall have concurrent power to enforce this article by appropriate legislation.

Section 3.
This article shall be inoperative unless it shall have been ratified as an amendment to the Constitution by the legislatures of the several States, as provided in the Constitution, within seven years from the date of the submission hereof to the States by the Congress.]
(Repealed by amendment 21)

Amendment XIX

Passed by Congress June 4, 1919. Ratified August 18, 1920.

The right of citizens of the United States to vote shall not be denied or abridged by the United States or by any State on account of sex.

Congress shall have power to enforce this article by appropriate legislation.

Amendment XX

Passed by Congress March 2, 1932. Ratified January 23, 1933.

Section 1.
The terms of the President and the Vice President shall end at noon on the 20th day of January, and the terms of Senators and Representatives at noon on the 3rd day of January, of the years in which such terms would have ended if this article had not been ratified; and the terms of their successors shall then begin.

Section 2.
The Congress shall assemble at least once in every year, and such meeting shall begin at noon on the 3d day of January, unless they shall by law appoint a different day.

Section 3.
If, at the time fixed for the beginning of the term of the President, the President elect shall have died, the Vice President elect shall become President. If a President shall not have been chosen before the time

fixed for the beginning of his term, or if the President elect shall have failed to qualify, then the Vice President elect shall act as President until a President shall have qualified; and the Congress may by law provide for the case wherein neither a President elect nor a Vice President shall have qualified, declaring who shall then act as President, or the manner in which one who is to act shall be selected, and such person shall act accordingly until a President or Vice President shall have qualified.

Section 4.
The Congress may by law provide for the case of the death of any of the persons from whom the House of Representatives may choose a President whenever the right of choice shall have devolved upon them, and for the case of the death of any of the persons from whom the Senate may choose a Vice President whenever the right of choice shall have devolved upon them.

Section 5.
Sections 1 and 2 shall take effect on the 15th day of October following the ratification of this article.

Section 6.
This article shall be inoperative unless it shall have been ratified as an amendment to the Constitution by the legislatures of three-fourths of the several States within seven years from the date of its submission.

Amendment XXI

Passed by Congress February 20, 1933. Ratified December 5, 1933.

Section 1.
The eighteenth article of amendment to the Constitution of the United States is hereby repealed.

Section 2.
The transportation or importation into any State, Territory, or Possession of the United States for delivery or use therein of intoxicating liquors, in violation of the laws thereof, is hereby prohibited.

Section 3.
This article shall be inoperative unless it shall have been ratified as an amendment to the Constitution by conventions in the several States, as provided in the Constitution, within seven years from the date of the submission hereof to the States by the Congress.

Amendment XXII

Passed by Congress March 21, 1947. Ratified February 27, 1951.

Section 1.
No person shall be elected to the office of the President more than twice, and no person who has held the office of President, or acted as President, for more than two years of a term to which some other

person was elected President shall be elected to the office of President more than once. But this Article shall not apply to any person holding the office of President when this Article was proposed by Congress, and shall not prevent any person who may be holding the office of President, or acting as President, during the term within which this Article becomes operative from holding the office of President or acting as President during the remainder of such term.

Section 2.
This article shall be inoperative unless it shall have been ratified as an amendment to the Constitution by the legislatures of three-fourths of the several States within seven years from the date of its submission to the States by the Congress.

Amendment XXIII

Passed by Congress June 16, 1960. Ratified March 29, 1961.

Section 1.
The District constituting the seat of Government of the United States shall appoint in such manner as Congress may direct:

A number of electors of President and Vice President equal to the whole number of Senators and Representatives in Congress to which the District would be entitled if it were a State, but in no event more than the least populous State; they shall be in addition to those appointed by the States, but they shall be considered, for the purposes of the election of President and Vice President, to be electors appointed by a State; and they shall meet in the District and perform such duties as provided by the twelfth article of amendment.

Section 2.
The Congress shall have power to enforce this article by appropriate legislation.

Amendment XXIV

Passed by Congress August 27, 1962. Ratified January 23, 1964.

Section 1.
The right of citizens of the United States to vote in any primary or other election for President or Vice President, for electors for President or Vice President, or for Senator or Representative in Congress, shall not be denied or abridged by the United States or any State by reason of failure to pay poll tax or other tax.

Section 2.
The Congress shall have power to enforce this article by appropriate legislation.

Amendment XXV

Passed by Congress July 6, 1965. Ratified February 10, 1967.

Section 1.
In case of the removal of the President from office or of his death or resignation, the Vice President shall become President.

Section 2.
Whenever there is a vacancy in the office of the Vice President, the President shall nominate a Vice President who shall take office upon confirmation by a majority vote of both Houses of Congress.

Section 3.
Whenever the President transmits to the President pro tempore of the Senate and the Speaker of the House of Representatives his written declaration that he is unable to discharge the powers and duties of his office, and until he transmits to them a written declaration to the contrary, such powers and duties shall be discharged by the Vice President as Acting President.

Section 4.
Whenever the Vice President and a majority of either the principal officers of the executive departments or of such other body as Congress may by law provide, transmit to the President pro tempore of the Senate and the Speaker of the House of Representatives

their written declaration that the President is unable to discharge the powers and duties of his office, the Vice President shall immediately assume the powers and duties of the office as Acting President.

Thereafter, when the President transmits to the President pro tempore of the Senate and the Speaker of the House of Representatives his written declaration that no inability exists, he shall resume the powers and duties of his office unless the Vice President and a majority of either the principal officers of the executive department or of such other body as Congress may by law provide, transmit within four days to the President pro tempore of the Senate and the Speaker of the House of Representatives their written declaration that the President is unable to discharge the powers and duties of his office. Thereupon Congress shall decide the issue, assembling within forty-eight hours for that purpose if not in session. If the Congress, within twenty-one days after receipt of the latter written declaration, or, if Congress is not in session, within twenty-one days after Congress is required to assemble, determines by two-thirds vote of both Houses that the President is unable to discharge the powers and duties of his office, the Vice President shall continue to discharge the same as Acting President; otherwise, the President shall resume the powers and duties of his office.

Amendment XXVI

Passed by Congress March 23, 1971. Ratified July 1, 1971.

Section 1.
The right of citizens of the United States, who are eighteen years of age or older, to vote shall not be denied or abridged by the United States or by any State on account of age.

Section 2.
The Congress shall have power to enforce this article by appropriate legislation.

Amendment XXVII

Originally proposed Sept. 25, 1789. Ratified May 7, 1992.

No law, varying the compensation for the services of the Senators and Representatives, shall take effect, until an election of representatives shall have intervened.

Note: Congress submitted the text of the Twenty-Seventh Amendment to the States as part of the proposed Bill of Rights on September 25, 1789. The Amendment was not ratified together with the first Ten Amendments, which became effective on December 15, 1791. The Twenty-Seventh Amendment was ratified on May 7, 1992, by the vote of Michigan.

• Veto of federal public works bill

March 3, 1817

To the House of Representatives of the United States:

Having considered the bill this day presented to me entitled "An act to set apart and pledge certain funds for internal improvements," and which sets apart and pledges funds "for constructing roads and canals, and improving the navigation of water courses, in order to facilitate, promote, and give security to internal commerce among the several States, and to render more easy and less expensive the means and provisions for the common defense," I am constrained by the insuperable difficulty I feel in reconciling the bill with the Constitution of the United States to return it with that objection to the House of Representatives, in which it originated.

The legislative powers vested in Congress are specified and enumerated in the eighth section of the first article of the Constitution, and it does not appear that the power proposed to be exercised by the bill is among the enumerated powers, or that it falls by any just interpretation with the power to make laws necessary and proper for carrying into execution those or other powers vested by the Constitution in the Government of the United States.

"The power to regulate commerce among the several States" can not include a power to construct roads and canals, and to improve the navigation of water courses in order to facilitate, promote, and secure such commerce without a latitude of construction departing from the ordinary import of the terms strengthened by the known inconveniences which doubtless led to the grant of this remedial power to Congress.

To refer the power in question to the clause "to provide for common defense and general welfare" would be contrary to the established and consistent rules of interpretation, as rendering the special and careful enumeration of powers which follow the clause nugatory and improper. Such a view of the Constitution would have the effect of giving to Congress a general power of legislation instead of the defined and limited one hitherto understood to belong to them, the terms "common defense and general welfare" embracing every object and act within the purview of a legislative trust. It would have the effect of subjecting both the Constitution and laws of the several States in all cases not specifically exempted to be superseded by laws of Congress, it being expressly declared "that the Constitution of the United States and laws made in pursuance thereof shall be the supreme law of the land, and the judges of every state shall be bound thereby, anything in the constitution or laws of any State to the contrary notwithstanding." Such a view of the Constitution, finally, would have the effect of excluding the judicial authority of the United States from its participation in guarding the boundary between the legislative powers of the General and the State Governments, inasmuch as questions relating to the general welfare, being questions of policy and expediency, are unsusceptible of judicial cognizance and decision.

A restriction of the power "to provide for the common defense and general welfare" to cases which are to be provided for by the expenditure of money would still leave within the legislative power of Congress all the great and most important measures of Government, money being the ordinary and necessary means of carrying them into execution.

If a general power to construct roads and canals, and to improve the navigation of water courses, with the train of powers incident thereto, be not possessed by Congress, the assent of the States in the mode provided in the bill can not confer the power. The only cases in which the consent and cession of particular States can extend the power of Congress are those specified and provided for in the Constitution.

I am not unaware of the great importance of roads and canals and the improved navigation of water courses, and that a power in the National Legislature to provide for them might be exercised with signal advantage to the general prosperity. But seeing that such a power is not expressly given by the Constitution, and believing that it can not be deduced from any part of it without an inadmissible latitude of construction and reliance on insufficient precedents; believing also that the permanent success of the Constitution depends on a definite partition of powers between the General and the State Governments, and that no adequate landmarks would be left by the constructive extension of the powers of Congress as proposed in the bill, I have no option but to withhold my signature from it, and to cherishing the hope that its beneficial objects may be attained by a resort for the necessary powers to the same wisdom and virtue in the nation which established the Constitution in its actual form and providently marked out in the instrument itself a safe and practicable mode of improving it as experience might suggest.

James Madison,

President of the United States

• Bibliography

• The List That Could Have Been

1. Thomas J. DiLorenzo, *Hamilton's Curse: How Jefferson's Arch Enemy Betrayed the American Revolution - And What It Means For Americans Today* (New York: Three Rivers Press, 2008) p. 22

2. A. Ralph Epperson, *The Unseen Hand: An Introduction to the Conspiratorial View of History* (Tucson, AZ: Publius Press, 1985) p. 139-140

3. Timothy L. Hall, *Supreme Court Justices: A Biographical Dictionary* (New York: Facts On File, Inc., 2001) p. 8

4. Alexander Hamilton, "Federalist Paper #78," Avalon Project, http://avalon.law.yale.edu/18th_century/fed78.asp#1 [accessed February 9, 2018]

5. Alexander Hamilton, James Madison, and John Jay, *The Federalist* (New York: The Modern Library – Random House Books, 1937)

6. A. Ralph Epperson, *The Unseen Hand: An Introduction to the Conspiratorial View of*

History (Tucson, AZ: Publius Press, 1985) p. 99-100

7. G. Edward Griffin, The Creature from Jekyll Island: A Second Look at the Federal Reserve (Westlake Village, CA: American Media, 1998) p. 24

8. Victor Lasky, It Didn't Start with Watergate (New York: Dell Publishing, 1977) p. 10

9. The Socialist Party of America, "Document Download Page (1906-1916)," https://www.marxists.org/history/usa/eam/spa/spadownloads-1906-1916.html [accessed February 9, 2018]

10. Peter Dreier, "The Fifty Most Influential Progressives of the Twentieth Century," *The Nation*, September 15, 2010; https://www.thenation.com/article/fifty-most-influential-progressives-twentieth-century [accessed February 9, 2018]

11. Ibid.

12. The Radiance Foundation, "The Mother of Planned Parenthood," *Too Many Aborted*, http://www.toomanyaborted.com/sanger/ [accessed February 9, 2018]

13. Diane S. Dew, "Margaret Sanger Founder of Planned Parenthood In Her Own Words," 2001; http://dianedew.com/sanger.htm [accessed February 9, 2018]

14. Peter Dreier, "The Fifty Most Influential Progressives of the Twentieth Century," *The Nation*, September 15, 2010; https://www.thenation.com/article/fifty-most-

influential-progressives-twentieth-century
[accessed February 9, 2018]

15.   Catholics 4 Trump, "Hillary Clinton 'In Awe
Of' and 'Enormously Admires' a Racist
Anti-Catholic Bigot," August 7, 2016;
https://www.catholics4trump.com/hillary-
clinton-in-awe-of-and-admires-enormously-
a-racist-anti-catholic-bigot/ [accessed
February 9, 2018]

16.   Peter Dreier, "The Fifty Most Influential
Progressives of the Twentieth Century," *The
Nation*, September 15, 2010;
https://www.thenation.com/article/fifty-most-
influential-progressives-twentieth-century
[accessed February 9, 2018]

17.   Brian Anderson, "ACLU Upset That Obama
Won't Exceed His Authority More,"
DownTrend, December 8, 2014;
https://downtrend.com/71superb/aclu-upset-
that-obama-wont-exceed-his-authority-more
[accessed February 9, 2018]

18.   Peter Dreier, "The Fifty Most Influential
Progressives of the Twentieth Century," *The
Nation*, September 15, 2010;
https://www.thenation.com/article/fifty-most-
influential-progressives-twentieth-century
[accessed February 9, 2018]

19.   Ibid.

20.   Ibid.

21.   New [one] World Order Quotes,
https://www.nationallibertyalliance.org/files/
quotes/NWO%20Quotes.pdf [accessed

February 9, 2018]

22. Margo Louis, "Why You Need To Know Saul," *The Founding Project*, June 2, 2017; https://thefoundingproject.com/need-know-saul [accessed February 9, 2018]

23. Peter Dreier, "The Fifty Most Influential Progressives of the Twentieth Century," *The Nation*, September 15, 2010; https://www.thenation.com/article/fifty-most-influential-progressives-twentieth-century [accessed February 9, 2018]

24. Reynolds v. Sims – Significance, http://law.jrank.org/pages/25430/Reynolds-v-Sims-Significance.html [accessed February 9, 2018]

25. Peter Dreier, "The Fifty Most Influential Progressives of the Twentieth Century," *The Nation*, September 15, 2010; https://www.thenation.com/article/fifty-most-influential-progressives-twentieth-century [accessed February 9, 2018]

26. David Greenberg, "Agit-Prof: Howard Zinn's influential mutilations of American History", *The New Republic*, March 18, 2013; https://newrepublic.com/article/112574/howard-zinns-influential-mutilations-american-history [accessed February 9, 2018]

27. World Heritage Encyclopedia, "Henry Kissinger," http://self.gutenberg.org/articles/eng/Henry_Kissinger [accessed February 9, 2018]

28. Anonymous Patriots, "Henry Kissinger –

Public Enemy #1 – And His Lawless Reign Over America," *American Intelligence Media*, March 14, 2017; https://aim4truth.org/2017/03/14/henry-kissinger-public-enemy-1-and-his-lawless-reign-over-america/ [accessed February 9, 2018]

29. Robin Langley Sommer, *The Presidents of the United States*, (New York: Dove Tail Books, 1997) p. 61

30. Richard McKenzie, *We the People: A Christian Nation*, (Bloomington, IN: Author House, 2010) p. 288

31. "Washington's Farewell Address," *The Lehrman Institute*, http://lehrmaninstitute.org/history/farewell-address.html [accessed February 10, 2018]

32. Robert Kagan, *Dangerous Nation*, (New York: Vintage Books, 2007)

33. Orville V. Webster, The Book of Presidents, (Los Angeles: JBG Publishing, 1991) p. 117

34. "The Nobel Peace Prize 2002," *Nobel Media*, https://www.nobelprize.org/nobel_prizes/peace/laureates/2002/ [accessed February 10, 2018]

35. Peter G. Bourne, *Jimmy Carter: A Comprehensive Biography From Plains to Post-Presidency*, (New York: Scribner, 1997) p. 44-55.

36. Andrew Glass, "Carter pardons draft dodgers Jan. 21, 1977," *Politico*, January 21, 2008; https://www.politico.com/story/2008/01/carte

r-pardons-draft-dodgers-jan-21-1977-007974 [accessed February 10, 2018]

37. Jimmy Carter: U.S. President, *The American Assembly: Columbia University*, http://americanassembly.org/people/awardee/ jimmy-carter [accessed February 10, 2018]

38. Iran-U.S Hostage Crisis (1979-1981), *The History Guy*, https://www.historyguy.com/iran-us_hostage_crisis.html#.WqTI3ujwZPY [accessed February 10, 2018]

39. Jimmy Carter, *Wikipedia*, https://en.wikipedia.org/wiki/Jimmy_Carter [accessed February 10, 2018]

40. A. Ralph Epperson, *The Unseen Hand: An Introduction to the Conspiratorial View of History* (Tucson, AZ: Publius Press, 1985) p. 232

41. Muchena Zigomo, "Annan, Carter say barred from Zimbabwe," *Reuters*, November 22, 2008; https://www.reuters.com/article/us-zimbabwe-politics-annan/annan-carter-say-barred-from-zimbabwe-idUSTRE4AL19320081122 [accessed February 10, 2018]

42. 1979 Soviet invasion of Afghanistan, *Revolvy*, https://www.revolvy.com/topic/1979%20Sov iet%20invasion%20of%20Afghanistan&item _type=topic [accessed February 10, 2018]

43. Frank Van Riper, "Carter calls for U.S. boycott of Olympics in Moscow in 1980,"

Daily News, January 20, 2016 (reprint of original article written January 21, 1980); http://www.nydailynews.com/news/national/carter-calls-u-s-boycott-olympics-moscow-1980-article-1.2503536 [accessed February 10, 2018]

44.   Richard Kruger, "The Nicaraguan Connection: A Threat to Central America," *The Heritage Foundation*, February 24, 1982; https://www.heritage.org/americas/report/the-nicaraguan-connection-threat-central-america [accessed February 10, 2018]

45.   Anders, "Zbigniew Brzezinski: Evil Spirit of 5 U.S. Presidents – and Biggest Threat to World Peace," https://www.bibliotecapleyades.net/sociopolitica/sociopol_brzezinski06.htm [accessed February 10, 2018]

46.   Kristian Smith, "Noam Chomsky: As Long As The Public is Under Control, Everything is Fine," *World News Daily Information Clearing House*, January 28, 2011; http://www.informationclearinghouse.info/article27369.htm [accessed February 10, 2018]

47.   Peter Dreier, "The Fifty Most Influential Progressives of the Twentieth Century," *The Nation*, September 15, 2010; https://www.thenation.com/article/fifty-most-influential-progressives-twentieth-century [accessed February 9, 2018]

48.   Ibid.

49.   Ibid.

50.   AWR Hawkins, "Alan Dershowitz on 2nd
       Amendment: 'An Absurd Thing' In Our
       Constitution," *Ammoland Shooting Sports
       News*, July 28, 2015;
       https://www.ammoland.com/2015/07/alan-
       dershowitz-2nd-amendment-an-absurd-thing-
       in-our-constitution/#axzz579llaQPE
       [accessed February 14, 2018]

51.   Nan Rubin, "Campus Profile: Alan
       Dershowitz," *Political Research Associates*,
       https://www.politicalresearch.org/campus-
       profile-alan-dershowitz/ [accessed February
       11, 2018]

52.   The New Yorker, "The Comey Testimony
       Live Blog: What the Former F.B.I. Director
       Said About Trump," *The New Yorker*, June 8,
       2017;
       https://www.newyorker.com/news/news-
       desk/the-comey-testimony-live-blog-what-
       will-he-reveal-about-trump [accessed
       February 14, 2018]

53.   Julie Pace, "White House defends contacts
       with FBI over Russia reports," *The Times of
       Israel*, February 25, 2017;
       http://www.timesofisrael.com/dershowitz-
       threatens-to-leave-democratic-party-if-
       ellison-elected-dnc-
       chair/?fb_comment_id=1105543429571720_
       1105974289528634#f29227ac8f9db38
       [accessed February 11, 2018]

54.   Peter Dreier, "The Fifty Most Influential

Progressives of the Twentieth Century," *The Nation*, September 15, 2010; https://www.thenation.com/article/fifty-most-influential-progressives-twentieth-century [accessed February 11, 2018]

55. A&E Television Networks, "Bernie Sanders Biography," *The Biography.com website*, February 22, 2018; https://www.biography.com/people/bernie-sanders-02032016 [accessed February 11, 2018]

56. Jedediah Purdy, "Bernie Sanders's New Deal Socialism," *The New Yorker*, November 20, 2015; https://www.newyorker.com/news/news-desk/bernie-sanderss-new-deal-socialism [accessed February 14, 2018]

57. Wikipedia, "Bernie Sanders," *Wikipedia*, https://en.wikipedia.org/wiki/Bernie_Sanders , [accessed February 11, 2018]

58. Gregory Cowles, "The Story Behind This Week's Best Sellers," *New York Times*, November 25, 2016; https://www.nytimes.com/2016/11/25/books/review/the-story-behind-this-weeks-best-sellers.html?_r=0 [accessed February 11, 2018]

59. Chomsky, Noam (2016-01-29), "Noam Chomsky on Clinton vs Sanders," *UpFront (Interview), Interview with Mehdi Hasan*, Boston, MA: Al Jazeera English; https://www.youtube.com/watch?v=btJfkPB

LULg [accessed February 11, 2018]

60. Jesse Jackson, "JACKSON: Right to vote needs constitutional protection," *Chicago Sun Times*, September 18, 2017; https://chicago.suntimes.com/columnists/jackson-right-to-vote-needs-constitutional-protection/ [accessed February 11, 2018]

61. Alexis de Tocqueville, *Democracy in America* (New York: The Colonial Press, 1900) p. 364

62. Zocalo Public Square, "Women and the Myth of the American West," *TIME*, January 11, 2015; http://time.com/3662361/women-american-west/ [accessed February 11, 2018]

63. Terresa Monroe-Hamilton, "Big Names Headline The People's Summit In Chicago – It's A Who's Who of Communists," *Trevor Loudon Presents New Zeal: Shining the Torch for Liberty*, March 28, 2017; http://www.trevorloudon.com/2017/03/big-names-headline-the-peoples-summit-in-chicago-its-a-whos-who-of-communists/?utm_source=akdart [accessed February 14, 2018]

64. Cynthia Weber, *Imagining America at War: Morality, politics, and film*, (New York: Routledge, 2006) p. 133-148

65. Michael Moore (October 8, 2009), "Michael Moore Talks About Socialism," *American Film Institute*, Silver Spring, MD: AFI Silver Theatre regarding CAPITALISM: A LOVE STORY; https://youtu.be/neyMdjrbM18

[accessed February 11, 2018]
66. Trevor Loudon, *The Enemies Within: Columnists, Socialists and Progressives in the U.S. Congress*, (Las Vegas: Pacific Freedom Foundation, 2013)

- **Honorable Mention: Theodore Roosevelt & Woodrow Wilson**

1. John D. Buenker, John C. Burnham, and Robert M. Crunden, *Progressivism* (Piscataway, NJ: Transaction Publishers, 1986) p. 3–21
2. Hedwig Richter (2016) Transactional Reform and Democracy: Election Reforms in New York City and Berlin around 1900. *The Journal of the Gilded Age and Progressive Era Volume 15, Issue 2*, pages 149-175
3. Henry J. Sage, "The Progressive Era: The Great Age Of Reform," *Sage American History*, 2012, 2017; http://sageamericanhistory.net/progressive/topics/progressive.html [accessed February 11, 2018]
4. Economic Policy, "The History of Economic Policy," Lumen: Boundless Political Science, https://courses.lumenlearning.com/boundless-politicalscience/chapter/the-history-of-economic-policy/ [accessed February 11, 2018]
5. Sidney M. Milkis, "The Transformation of American Democracy: Teddy Roosevelt, the

1912 Election, and the Progressive Party,"
The Heritage Foundation, June 11, 2012;
https://www.heritage.org/political-
process/report/the-transformation-american-
democracy-teddy-roosevelt-the-1912-election
[accessed February 11, 2018]

6.   Christopher Burkett, "Remaking the World:
Progressivism and American Foreign
Policy," The Heritage Foundation, September
24, 2013; https://www.heritage.org/political-
process/report/remaking-the-world-
progressivism-and-american-foreign-policy
[accessed February 11, 2018]

7.   Thomas J. DiLorenzo, *Hamilton's Curse:
How Jefferson's Arch Enemy Betrayed the
American Revolution - And What It Means
For Americans Today* (New York: Three
Rivers Press, 2008) p. 22

8.   Richard Hofstadter, *The American Political
Tradition and the Men Who Made It* (New
York: Vintage Books, 1948) p. 286

9.   Mark Hitchcock, *The Late Great United
States* (Colorado Springs: Multnomah Books,
2010) p. 89

10.   James Madison, "The Federalist Papers: No.
45 – The Alleged Danger From the Powers of
the Union to the State Governments
Considered For the Independent Fournal,"
The Avalon Project – Yale Law School;
http://avalon.law.yale.edu/18th_century/fed4
5.asp [accessed February 11, 2018]

11.   NCC Staff, "A quick look at Thomas

Jefferson's constitutional legacy," *Constitution Daily, National Constitution Center*, November 24, 2015; https://constitutioncenter.org/blog/a-quick-look-at-thomas-jeffersons-constitutional-legacy/ [accessed February 11, 2018]

12. Dumas Malone, *Jefferson The President: First Term 1801-1805*, (Boston: Little, Brown and Company, 1970) p. 111

13. Thomas Jefferson (1854). *"The writings of Thomas Jefferson: being his autobiography, correspondence, reports, messages, addresses, and other writings, official and private"*, p.453

14. Thomas Jefferson, "From Thomas Jefferson To William Johnson, 12 June 1823," *Founders Online, National Archives*; https://founders.archives.gov/documents/Jefferson/98-01-02-3562 [accessed February 11, 2018]

15. James Madison, "Madison's Veto of the Federal Public Works Bill, 1817," *Political Pistachio*, February 18, 2018; http://politicalpistachio.blogspot.com/2018/02/madisons-veto-of-federal-public-works.html

16. Kenneth Dautrich, David A. Yalof, Christina Bejarano, *The Enduring Democracy* (Boston: Cengage Learning, 2018) p. 180

17. Christopher H. Pyle and Richard M. Pious, *The President, Congress, and the Constitution: Power and Legitimacy in*

American Politics (New York: The Free
Press, 1984) p. 69

18. Theodore Roosevelt, *An Autobiography*
(New York: The MacMillan Company, 1916)
p. 372

19. Jeff Nilsson, "1912: A Chaotic Presidential
Election," *The Saturday Evening Post*,
November 3, 2012;
http://www.saturdayeveningpost.com/2012/1
1/03/history/post-perspective/1912-
election.html [accessed February 7, 2018]

20. Dan Schlenoff, "Before America Joined the
Great War," *Scientific American*, April 1,
2017;
https://www.scientificamerican.com/article/w
ar-opinions/ [accessed February 11, 2018]

21. Matthew A. Crenson and Benjamin Ginsberg,
*Presidential Power: Unchecked and
Unbalanced* (New York: W.W. Norton &
Company, 2007) p. 221-222

22. Henry Campbell Black, M.A., *Black's Law
Dictionary* (St. Paul, MN: West Publishing
Co., 1991) p.593

23. "The WTO and GATT: A Principled
History," *The Brookings Institute*,
https://www.brookings.edu/wp-
content/uploads/2016/07/selfenforcingtrade_
chapter.pdf [accessed February 9, 2018]

24. History.com Staff, "Woodrow Wilson suffers
a stroke," *History.com-A&E Networks*, 2009;
https://www.history.com/this-day-in-
history/woodrow-wilson-suffers-a-stroke

[accessed February 11, 2018]

25. Woodrow Wilson, "President Woodrow Wilson's Fourteen Points," *The Avalon Project – Yale Law School,* January 8, 1918 (2008); http://avalon.law.yale.edu/20th_century/wilson14.asp [accessed February 14, 2018]

26. Robin Langley Sommer, *The Presidents of the United States* (New York: Barnes & Noble Books, 1997) p. 41

27. Sidney Lens, *The Forging of the American Empire* (New York: Thomas Y. Crowell Company 1974) p. 286

28. Meg Sullivan, "FDR's policies prolonged Depression by 7 years, UCLA economists calculate," *UCLA Newsroom*, August 10, 2004; http://newsroom.ucla.edu/releases/FDR-s-Policies-Prolonged-Depression-5409 [accessed February 16, 2018]

29. Kathleen Dalton, *Theodore Roosevelt: A Strenuous Life* (New York: Vintage Books, 2002) p. 513

• 1. Alexander Hamilton

1. Robert Kagan, "Our 'Messianic Impulse,'" *Washington Post*, December 10, 2006; http://www.washingtonpost.com/wp-dyn/content/article/2006/12/08/AR2006120801516.html [accessed February 11, 2018]

2. Thomas J. DiLorenzo, *Hamilton's Curse:*

How Jefferson's Arch Enemy Betrayed the American Revolution - And What It Means For Americans Today (New York: Three Rivers Press, 2008) p. 178-179

3. William V. Wells, *The life and public service of Samuel Adams* (Boston: Little, Brown and Company, 1865) Volume I, p. 154

4. W. Cleon Skousen, *The 5000 Year Leap* (Washington D.C.: National Center for Constitution Studies, 2006) p. 30

5. Thomas J. DiLorenzo, *Hamilton's Curse: How Jefferson's Arch Enemy Betrayed the American Revolution - And What It Means For Americans Today* (New York: Three Rivers Press, 2008) p. 20-23

6. Ibid.

7. Ibid.

8. Ibid.

9. Real Clear Politics, "Bloomberg On Soda Ban: 'We're Simply Forcing You To Understand,'" *Real Clear Politics*, May 31, 2012; https://www.realclearpolitics.com/video/2012/05/31/bloomberg_on_sad_ban_were_simply_forcing_you_to_understand.html [accessed February 16, 2018]

10. L. Peter Schultz, *Governing America* (New York: University Press, 1997) p. 12

11. Ronald J. Pestritto and Thomas G. West, ed. *Challenges to the American Founding: Slavery, Historicism, and Progressivism in the Nineteenth Century*, (New York:

Lexington Books, 2005) p. 10-11

12. Akhil Reed Amar, *America's Constitution: A Biography* (New York: Random House, 2005) p. 142

13. Virginia v. Maryland, 540 U.S. 56 (2003). https://www.law.cornell.edu/supremecourt/text/129ORIG [accessed February 11, 2018]

14. Jay A. Parry, Andrew M. Allison and W. Cleon Skousen, *The Real George Washington*, (Washington D.C.: National Center for Constitutional Studies, 2010) p. 450

15. Catherine Drinker Bowen, *Miracle At Philadelphia: The Story of the Constitutional Convention, May to September 1787* (Boston: Little, Brown and Company, 1966) p. 8-9

16. Alexander Hamilton, James Madison, and John Jay, *The Federalist* (New York: The Modern Library – Random House Books, 1937)

17. Clinton Rossiter, *Alexander Hamilton and the Constitution* (New York: Harcourt Brace, 1964) p. 27-28

18. Thomas J. DiLorenzo, *Hamilton's Curse: How Jefferson's Arch Enemy Betrayed the American Revolution - And What It Means For Americans Today* (New York: Three Rivers Press, 2008) p. 11

19. Alexander Hamilton, "Alexander Hamilton to Gouverneur Morris, January 27, 1802," *Alexander Hamilton: The Man Who Made Modern America*;

http://www.alexanderhamiltonexhibition.org/
letters/01_27.html [accessed February 11,
2018]

20.   Thomas J. DiLorenzo, *Hamilton's Curse:
How Jefferson's Arch Enemy Betrayed the
American Revolution - And What It Means
For Americans Today* (New York: Three
Rivers Press, 2008) p. 40

21.   Ibid. p. 49

22.   Ibid. p. 51

23.   William Graham Sumner, *Alexander
Hamilton*, (New York: Dodd, Mead, and
Company, 1890) p. 162,

24.   Thomas J. DiLorenzo, *Hamilton's Curse:
How Jefferson's Arch Enemy Betrayed the
American Revolution - And What It Means
For Americans Today* (New York: Three
Rivers Press, 2008) p. 104-105

25.   Ibid. p. 59-61

26.   Theodore Roosevelt, *An Autobiography*
(New York: Charles Scribner's Sons, 1922)
p. 357

27.   Thomas J. DiLorenzo, *Hamilton's Curse:
How Jefferson's Arch Enemy Betrayed the
American Revolution - And What It Means
For Americans Today* (New York: Three
Rivers Press, 2008) p. 26

28.   Ibid. p. 62

29.   Clinton Rosserter, *Alexander Hamilton and
the Constitution* (New York: Harcourt Brace,
1964) p. 237

30.   Dumas Malone, *Jefferson The President:*

First Term 1801-1805 (Boston: Little, Brown
and Company, 1970) p. 116

31.   Philip B. Kurland and Ralph Lerner, ed., *The
Founders' Constitution, Volume Four,
Article 2, Section 2, through Article 7*
(Indianapolis: Liberty Fund, 1987) p. 165

• 2. John Marshall

1.   Jean Edward Smith, *John Marshall: Definer
of a Nation* (New York: Henry Holt and
Company, 1996) p. 117
2.   Hugh Blair Grigsby, *History of the Virginia
Federal Convention of 1788* (New York: Da
Capo Press, 1969)
3.   Jean Edward Smith, *John Marshall: Definer
of a Nation* (New York: Henry Holt and
Company, 1996) p. 131
4.   Ibid. p. 132
5.   Ibid.
6.   McCulloch v. Maryland, 17 U.S. 4 (1819).
7.   St. George Tucker, *View of the Constitution
of the United States with Selected Writings
[1803]* (Indianapolis: Liberty Fund, Inc.,
1999) p. 32
8.   John Taylor, *Tyranny Unmasked*
(Washington City: Davis and Force, 1822) p.
258
9.   Marbury v. Madison, 5 U.S. 137 (1803).
10.   Ibid.
11.   Thomas J. DiLorenzo, *Hamilton's Curse:
How Jefferson's Arch Enemy Betrayed the*

American Revolution - And What It Means For Americans Today (New York: Three Rivers Press, 2008) p. 83

12. Ibid. p. 84
13. Coffman, Steve (2012). Words of the Founding Fathers. NC, USA: McFarland. p. 184. ISBN 978-0-7864-5862-2.
14. Newsweek Staff, "Why Marbury V. Madison Still Matters," *Newsweek*, February 20, 2009; http://www.newsweek.com/why-marbury-v-madison-still-matters-82263 [accessed February 13, 2018]
15. JRank, "United States v. Peters – The Fate of the Active," *Net Industries*, http://law.jrank.org/pages/25262/United-States-v-Peters-Fate-Active.html#ixzz3yBereUoz [accessed February 19, 2018]
16. Ibid.
17. Ibid.
18. Ibid.
19. Ibid.
20. Donald Scarinci, ed., "United States v. Peters & The Power of the Federal Courts," *Constitutional Law Reporter*, January 17, 2017; https://constitutionallawreporter.com/2017/01/17/historical-united-states-v-peters/ [Accessed February 19, 2018]
21. JRank, "United States v. Peters – To Prevent 'a Solemn Mockery,'" *Net Industries*, http://law.jrank.org/pages/25263/United-

States-v-Peters-Prevent-Solemn-Mockery.html [accessed February 19, 2018]

22. Fletcher v. Peck, 10 U.S. 87 (1810).

23. "Fletcher v. Peck (1810)", *Marshall Court Impact*, https://marshallcourtimpact.weebly.com/fletcher-v-peck-1810.html [accessed February 14, 2018]

24. Fletcher v. Peck, 10 U.S. 87 (1810).

25. Martin v. Hunter's Lessee, 14 U.S 304 (1816).

26. Dartmouth College Charter, *Dartmouth Library*, https://www.dartmouth.edu/~library/rauner/dartmouth/dc-charter.html [accessed February 19, 2018]

27. Christopher Muscato, "Dartmouth College v. Woodward: Summary & Overview," *Study.com*, https://study.com/academy/lesson/dartmouth-college-v-woodward-summary-lesson-quiz.html [accessed February 14, 2018]

28. Daniel Webster, "Select Speeches of Daniel Webster 1817-1845," *Project Gutenberg*, March 26, 2014, https://www.gutenberg.org/files/7600/7600-h/7600-h.htm [accessed February 19, 2018]

29. Dartmouth College v. Woodward, 17 U. S. 518 (1819)

30. Richard W. Morin, "Will to Resist: The Dartmouth College Case," *Dartmouth College*, April 1969,

https://files.eric.ed.gov/fulltext/ED097837.pd
f [accessed February 19, 2018]

31.   McCulloch v. Maryland, 17 U.S. 4 (1819).

32.   "McCulloch v. Maryland (1819)," *Bill of Rights Institute*,
http://www.billofrightsinstitute.org/educate/e
ducator-resources/lessons-plans/landmark-
supreme-court-cases-elessons/mcculloch-v-
maryland-1819/ [accessed February 19,
2018]

33.   McCulloch v. Maryland, 17 U.S. 4 (1819).

34.   "McCulloch v. Maryland (1819)," *Bill of Rights Institute*,
http://www.billofrightsinstitute.org/educate/e
ducator-resources/lessons-plans/landmark-
supreme-court-cases-elessons/mcculloch-v-
maryland-1819/ [accessed February 19,
2018]

35.   Ibid.

36.   Ibid.

37.   Cohens v. Virginia, 19 U.S. 264 (1821)

38.   Ibid.

39.   JRank, "Cohens v. Virginia – Significance," *Net Industries*,
http://law.jrank.org/pages/25264/Cohens-v-
Virginia-Significance.html [accessed
February 19, 2018]

40.   George Haskins, "John Marshall and the
Commerce Clause of the Constitution
[1955],"
University of Pennsylvania,
http://scholarship.law.upenn.edu/cgi/viewcon

tent.cgi?article=7434&context=penn_law_re
view [accessed February 16, 2018]
41. James Madison, "Madison Debates August
29, 1787, In Convention," The Avalon
Project, Yale Law School;
*http://avalon.law.yale.edu/18th_century/deba
tes_829.asp* [accessed February 16, 2018]
42. James Madison, "Madison Debates August
16, 1787, In Convention," The Avalon
Project, Yale Law School;
*http://avalon.law.yale.edu/18th_century/deba
tes_816.asp* [accessed February 16, 2018]
43. Philip B. Kurland and Ralph Lerner, ed., *The
Founders' Constitution, Volume Two,
Preamble through Article 1, Section 8,
Clause 4* (Indianapolis: Liberty Fund, 1987)
p. 517
44. "regulate." *Noah Webster's 1828 American
Dictionary of the English Language. 2018.*
https://1828.mshaffer.com/d/word/regulate
[accessed February 16, 2018]
45. Gibbons v. Ogden, 22 U.S. 1 (1824).
46. Ibid.
47. Ibid.
48. George Haskins, "John Marshall and the
Commerce Clause of the Constitution
[1955],"
University of Pennsylvania,
http://scholarship.law.upenn.edu/cgi/viewcon
tent.cgi?article=7434&context=penn_law_re
view [accessed February 16, 2018]
49. Wickard v. Filburn, 317 U.S. (1942)

50. Ibid.
51. Worcester v. Georgia, 31 U.S. 515 (1832)
52. Ibid.
53. Ibid.
54. Worcester v. Georgia – Significance, http://law.jrank.org/pages/25518/Worcester-v-Georgia-Significance.html [accessed February 17, 2018]
55. Ibid.
56. Ibid.
57. Worcester v. Georgia, 31 U.S. 515 (1832)
58. Jean Edward Smith, *John Marshall: Definer of a Nation (*New York: Henry Holt and Company, 1996) p. 518
59. "Indian Removal Act," *WikiVisually*, https://wikivisually.com/wiki/Indian_Removal_Act [accessed February 17, 2018]
60. Worcester v. Georgia – Significance, http://law.jrank.org/pages/25518/Worcester-v-Georgia-Significance.html [accessed February 17, 2018]
61. Barron v. Mayor & City Council of Baltimore, 32 U.S. 243 (1833)
62. "Did the 14th Amendment really incorporate the Bill of Rights?" *Constitution Mythbuster*, July 28, 2011; https://constitutionmythbuster.com/2011/07/28/did-the-14th-amendment-really-incorporate-the-bill-of-rights/ [accessed February 17, 2018]
63. Raoul Berger, *Incorporation of the Bill of Rights in the Fourteenth Amendment: A*

Nine-Lived Cat (Ohio State Law Journal, Moritz College of Law, vol. 42, no. 2, 1981) p. 435-466

• 3. Andrew Jackson

1. Orville Webster, *The Book of Presidents*, (Los Angeles: JBG Publishing, 1991) p. 29-30
2. Robin Langley Sommer, *The Presidents of the United States* (New York: Dove Tail Books, 1997) p. 17
3. Orville Webster, *The Book of Presidents*, (Los Angeles: JBG Publishing, 1991) p. 30
4. Daniel J. Boorstin, *The Americans: The Colonial Experience* (New York: Vintage Books, 1958) p. 205
5. Orville Webster, *The Book of Presidents*, (Los Angeles: JBG Publishing, 1991) p. 30
6. Robin Langley Sommer, *The Presidents of the United States* (New York: Dove Tail Books, 1997) p. 17
7. Rosemary and Stephen Vincent Benet, *A book of Americans* (New York: Rinehart & Co., 1933) p. 60-61
8. H.W. Brands, *Andrew Jackson: His Life and Times* (New York: Doubleday, 2005) p. 371
9. "Andrew Jackson, banks, and the Panic of 1837," Lehrman Institute, http://lehrmaninstitute.org/history/Andrew-Jackson-1837.html [accessed February 11, 2018]

10. A. Ralph Epperson, *The Unseen Hand: An Introduction to the Conspiratorial View of History* (Tucson, AZ: Publius Press, 1985) p. 134-135

11. A. Ralph Epperson, *The Unseen Hand: An Introduction to the Conspiratorial View of History* (Tucson, AZ: Publius Press, 1985) p. 135

12. Robert Remini, *The Revolutionary Age of Andrew Jackson* (New York: Avon Books, 1976) p. 128

13. James D. Richardson, *A Compilation of the Messages and Papers of the Presidents Volume II, Part 3: Andrew Jackson, March 4, 1829 to March 4, 1833*, p. 247/396

14. Robert V. Remini, *Andrew Jackson and the Course of American Democracy, 1833-1845* (Baltimore: The John Hopkins University Press, 1984) p. 480

15. Randall G. Holcombe, "Origins of the Electoral College," *Mises Institute: Austrian Economics, Freedom, and Peace*, November 9, 2000; https://mises.org/library/origins-electoral-college [accessed February 17, 2018]

16. Ibid.

17. John R. Koza, Barry F. Fadem, mark Grueskin, Michael S. Mandell, Robert Richie, and Joseph F. Zimmerman, *Every Vote Equal: A State-Based Plan for Electing the President by National Popular Vote* (Los Altos, CA: National Popular Vote Press,

2013) p. 360
18.   Ibid. p. 31
19.   Randall G. Holcombe, "Origins of the
       Electoral College," *Mises Institute: Austrian
       Economics, Freedom, and Peace*, November
       9, 2000; https://mises.org/library/origins-
       electoral-college [accessed February 17,
       2018]
20.   Mary Gabriel, "Who was Karl Marx?" *CNN*,
       October 29, 2011;
       CNN.http://edition.cnn.com/2011/10/29/opin
       ion/gabriel-karl-marx/index.html [accessed
       February 11, 2018]
21.   Douglas V. Gibbs, "But, What About The
       Will of the People?" *Political Pistachio*, May
       03, 2017;
       http://politicalpistachio.blogspot.com/2017/0
       5/but-what-about-will-of-people.html
       [accessed February 17, 2018]
22.   Randall G. Holcombe, "Origins of the
       Electoral College," *Mises Institute: Austrian
       Economics, Freedom, and Peace*, November
       9, 2000; https://mises.org/library/origins-
       electoral-college [accessed February 17,
       2018]

• 4. Joseph Story

1.   David Brion Davis, *Antebellum American
       culture* (University Park, PA: Pennsylvania
       State University Press, 1979) p. 14-15
2.   R. Kent Newmyer, *Supreme Court Justice*

Joseph Story: Statesman of the Old Republic (Chapel Hill: The University of North Carolina Press, 1985) p. 160

3.   Dunne, Gerald T., *Justice Joseph Story and the Rise of the Supreme Court* (New York: Simon & Schuster, 1970) p. 32

4.   Clare Cushman, *The Supreme Court Justices: Illustrated Biographies, 1789-2012* (Los Angeles: CQ Press, 2013) p. 76

5.   Ibid. p. 78

6.   Clinton Rossiter, *Alexander Hamilton and the Constitution* (New York: Harcourt Brace, 1964) p. 244

7.   Thomas J. DiLorenzo, *Hamilton's Curse: How Jefferson's Arch Enemy Betrayed the American Revolution - And What It Means For Americans Today* (New York: Three Rivers Press, 2008) p. 124

8.   Martin v. Hunter's Lessee, 14 U.S 304 (1816).

9.   Judge Douglass H. Bartley, *The Kiss of Judice: The Constitution Betrayed: A Coroner's Inquest and Report Volume 4* (Ely, MN: Judge Douglass H. Bartley, 2013) p. 209

10.   Ibid.

11.   McCulloch v. Maryland, 17 U.S. 4 (1819).

12.   William Loren Katz, *Breaking the Chains: African-American Slave Resistance* (New York: Collier Macmillan, 1990) p.121-122

13.   Ibid.

14.   Professor Douglas O. Linder, "The Amistad

Trials: An Account," *Famous Trials*, http://www.famous-trials.com/amistad/1241-account [accessed February 17, 2018]

15. Ibid.
16. Ibid.
17. Ibid.
18. Ibid.
19. Ibid.
20. Ibid.
21. Ibid.
22. Ibid.
23. Ibid.
24. Ibid.
25. Ibid.
26. Ibid.
27. "Josiah Willard Gibbs Sr.," *Wikipedia*, https://en.wikipedia.org/wiki/Josiah_Willard_Gibbs_Sr. [accessed February 11, 2018]
28. Douglas Linder (University of Missouri-Kansas City School of Law), "The Amistad Case," *Jurist*, June 2001; http://www.jurist.org/j20/famoustrials/the-amistad-case.php [accessed February 17, 2018]
29. Professor Douglas O. Linder, "The Amistad Trials: An Account," *Famous Trials*, http://www.famous-trials.com/amistad/1241-account [accessed February 17, 2018]
30. Ibid.
31. Ibid.
32. Ibid.
33. Ibid.

34. Ibid.
35. Ibid.
36. Ibid.
37. Ibid.
38. Ibid.
39. Ibid.
40. Douglas Linder (University of Missouri-Kansas City School of Law), "The Amistad Case," *Jurist*, June 2001; http://www.jurist.org/j20/famoustrials/the-amistad-case.php [accessed February 17, 2018]
41. Ibid.
42. Ibid.
43. Professor Douglas O. Linder, "The Amistad Trials: An Account," *Famous Trials*, http://www.famous-trials.com/amistad/1241-account [accessed February 17, 2018]
44. Ibid.
45. "Joseph Story," *Wikipedia*, https://en.wikipedia.org/wiki/Joseph_Story [accessed February 17, 2018]

• 5. Franklin Delano Roosevelt

1. Sturgess F. Cary, *Arrow Book of Presidents* (New York: Scholastic Book Services, 1976) p. 105
2. Earl Schenck Miers, ed., *The American Story: From Columbus to the Atom* (New York: Channel Press, 1956) p. 305
3. Samuel Rosenman, ed., *Franklin D.*

Roosevelt, Inaugural Address, March 4, 1933 – The Public Papers of Franklin D. Roosevelt, Volume Two: The Year of Crisis, 1933 (New York: Random House, 1938) p. 11–16

4.   Franklin D. Roosevelt, "Fireside Chat – March 9, 1937," *The American Presidency Project*, http://www.presidency.ucsb.edu/ws/index.php?pid=15381 [accessed February 18, 2018]

5.   Franklin D. Roosevelt, "Address of Franklin D. Roosevelt as Governor of New York, March 2, 1930," http://www.lexrex.com/enlightened/writings/fdr_address.htm [accessed February 18, 2018]

6.   Editors of Encyclopaedia Britannica, "United States presidential election of 1932," *Encyclopaedia Britannica*, https://www.britannica.com/event/United-States-presidential-election-of-1932 [accessed February 18, 2018]

7.   Franklin D. Roosevelt, "Fireside Chat – March 9, 1937," *The American Presidency Project*, http://www.presidency.ucsb.edu/ws/index.php?pid=15381 [accessed February 18, 2018]

8.   W. Cleon Skousen, *The Making of America: The Substance and Meaning of the Constitution* (Washington D.C.: The National Center for Constitutional Studies, 1985, 2007) p. 584

9. Samuel Rosenman, ed., *Franklin D. Roosevelt, Inaugural Address, March 4, 1933 – The Public Papers of Franklin D. Roosevelt, Volume Two: The Year of Crisis, 1933* (New York: Random House, 1938) p. 11–16

10. Joseph P. Lash, *Eleanor and Franklin* (New York: W.W. Norton and Company, Inc., 1971) p. 383

11. Ibid. p 383-384

12. Ernest Cassara, "Reformer as Politician: Horace Mann and the Anti-Slavery Struggle in Congress, 1848-1853." *Journal of American Studies 5 (December 1971)*

13. Jonathan Messerli, *Horace Mann: A Biography* (New York: Knopf, 1972) p. 247-264

14. "Regarding the friendly relationship and influences between progressives and Fabians," *Progressing America*, July 20, 2012; http://progressingamerica.blogspot.com/2012/07/regarding-friendly-relationship-and.html [accessed February 18, 2018]

15. *The American Fabian: Organ of Fabian Socialism in the United States (Volume III, No. 11)* (New York: The Fabian Educational Company, November 1897) p.4

16. "Regarding the friendly relationship and influences between progressives and Fabians," *Progressing America*, July 20, 2012;

http://progressingamerica.blogspot.com/2012
/07/regarding-friendly-relationship-and.html
[accessed February 18, 2018]

17. Richard Hofstadter, ed., *Great Issues in American History: From Reconstruction to the Present Day, 1864-1969* (New York: Random House, 1982) p. 384

18. Ibid. p. 394

19. Franklin D. Roosevelt, "Campaign Address at Cleveland, Ohio – November 2, 1940," *The American Presidency Project*, http://www.presidency.ucsb.edu/ws/?pid=15 893 [accessed February 18, 2018]

20. Franklin D. Roosevelt, "Message for American Education Week – September 27, 1938," *The American Presidency Project*, http://www.presidency.ucsb.edu/ws/?pid=15 545 [accessed February 18, 2018]

21. Brent McKee, "What Was The New Deal," *The Living New Deal*; https://livingnewdeal.org/what-was-the-new-deal/programs/ [accessed February 19, 2018]

22. David B. Woolner, "The New Deal's Unintended Impact on Education," *Roosevelt Institute*, September 9, 2010; http://rooseveltinstitute.org/new-deals-unintended-impact-education/ [accessed February 19, 2018]

23. Kevin R. Rosar, "Act to Establish a Federal Department of Education, 1867," *Federal Education Policy History*, 2001; (https://federaleducationpolicy.wordpress.co

m/2011/02/19/1867-act-to-establish-a-federal-department-of-education/) [accessed February 19, 2018]

24. "Education Department Created". United Press International. October 18, 1979.

25. John T. Flynn, *The Roosevelt Myth* (Garden City, N.Y.: Garden City Books, 1948) p. 77–78.

26. Gabriel Debenedetti, "Sanders invokes FDR to defend democratic socialism," *Politico*, November 19, 2015; https://www.politico.com/story/2015/11/bernie-sanders-socialism-speech-216071 [accessed February 19, 2018]

27. Katharine Q. Seelye, "Clinton Calls for 'Poverty Czar,'" New York Times, April 4, 2008; https://thecaucus.blogs.nytimes.com/2008/04/04/clinton-calls-for-poverty-czar/ [accessed February 19, 2018]

28. Michael Medved, *The 10 Big Lies About America*, (New York: Crown Forum, 2008) p. 142

29. Isaiah Berlin, *Karl Marx: Thoroughly Revised Fifth Edition,* (Princeton: Princeton University Press, 2013) p. 230

30. Michael Medved, *The 10 Big Lies About America*, (New York: Crown Forum, 2008) p. 147

31. Ibid. p. 150

32. Michael Medved, "How government expansion worsens hard times," *Townhall*,

October 24, 2007;
https://townhall.com/columnists/michaelmed
ved/2007/10/24/how-government-expansion-
worsens-hard-times-n799729 [accessed
February 19, 2018]

33.   Franklin Delano Roosevelt, "'Only Thing We
       Have to Fear is Fear Itself': FDR's First
       Inaugural Address," *History Matters –
       George Mason University*,
       http://historymatters.gmu.edu/d/5057
       [accessed February 19, 2018]

34.   "Franklin D. Roosevelt's First Inaugural
       Address," History.com – Speeches & Audio;
       http://www.history.com/speeches/franklin-d-
       roosevelts-first-inaugural-address [accessed
       February 11, 2018]

• 6. Lyndon B. Johnson

1.   Lisa Jardine, "Lyndon B. Johnson: The
       uncivil rights reformer," *Independent*,
       January 21, 2009;
       http://www.independent.co.uk/news/presiden
       ts/lyndon-b-johnson-the-uncivil-rights-
       reformer-1451816.html [accessed February
       28, 2018]

2.   John Daniel Davidson, "It's Time to Repeal
       the Johnson Amendment and Let Pastors
       Talk Politics," *The Federalist*, December 1,
       2017;
       http://thefederalist.com/2017/12/01/time-
       repeal-johnson-amendment-let-pastors-talk-

politics/ [accessed February 28, 2018]

3. Ibid.

4. Adam Serwer, "Lyndon Johnson was a civil rights hero. But also a racist.", *MSNBC*, April 12, 2014; http://www.msnbc.com/msnbc/lyndon-johnson-civil-rights-racism [accessed February 11, 2018]

5. Larry Schweikart and Michael Allen, *A Patriot's History of the United States: From Columbus's Great Discovery to the War on Terror* (New York: Sentinel, 2007) p. 683

6. Ibid.

7. Ibid.

8. David Barton, *Setting the Record Straight: American History in Black and White* (Aledo, TX: Wallbuilder Press; 2004) p. 129

9. John Fund, "Hillary's America – A Two-by-Four Bashing Democrats," *National Review*, July 18, 2016; *https://www.nationalreview.com/2016/07/hillarys-america-dinesh-dsouza-democrats-racist-past-corrupt-present/* [accessed February 20, 2018]

10. Dinesh D'Souza, "WND: Top 10 Highlights of Hillary's America," *D'Souza*, August 7, 2016; https://www.dineshdsouza.com/news/top-10-highlights/ [accessed February 11, 2018]

11. Ibid.

12. Jerome R. Corsi, PH.D., *America for Sale* (New York: Threshold Editions, 2009) p. 43

13. John Eberhard, "The Tytler Cycle Revisited," *Common Sense Government*, March 14, 2009 http://commonsensegovernment.com/the-tytler-cycle-revisited/ [accessed February 11, 2018]

14. A. Ralph Epperson, *The Unseen Hand: An Introduction to the Conspiratorial View of History* (Tucson, AZ: Publius Press, 1985) p. 47

15. Larken Rose, *The Most Dangerous Superstition* (Larken Rose; 2012) p.85-86

16. Translated by Jonathan Murphy and Mark Kramer, *The Black Book of Communism: Crimes, Terror, Repression* (Cambridge, MA: Harvard University Press, 1999) p. 605

17. Editors of Encyclopaedia Britannica, "Lyndon B. Johnson: President of United States," *Encyclopaedia Britannica*, https://www.britannica.com/biography/Lyndon-B-Johnson [accessed February 11, 2018]

18. "Lyndon B. Johnson and Ronald Reagan and Federal Power," *Bill of Rights Institute*, https://www.billofrightsinstitute.org/educate/educator-resources/lessons-plans/presidents-constitution/johnson-and-reagan/ [accessed February 11, 2018]

19. Ibid.

20. Editors of Encyclopaedia Britannica, "Lyndon B. Johnson: President of United States," *Encyclopaedia Britannica*, https://www.britannica.com/biography/Lyndon-B-Johnson [accessed February 11, 2018]

21. Ibid.
22. Lyndon B. Johnson, "Proclamation 3786 – Citizenship Day and Constitution Week, 1967; Mary 24, 1967," *The American Presidency Project, University of California at Santa Barbara*; http://www.presidency.ucsb.edu/ws/index.php?pid=106028 [accessed February 11, 2018]
23. Lyndon B. Johnson, "President Johnson's Special Message to the Congress: The American Promise (video and transcript) March 15, 1965," *LBJ Presidential Library*, http://www.lbjlibrary.org/lyndon-baines-johnson/speeches-films/president-johnsons-special-message-to-the-congress-the-american-promise [accessed February 11, 2018]
24. Ibid.
25. Ibid.
26. Adam Serwer, "Lyndon Johnson was a civil rights hero. But also a racist.", *MSNBC*, April 12, 2014; http://www.msnbc.com/msnbc/lyndon-johnson-civil-rights-racism [accessed February 11, 2018]
27. Lyndon B. Johnson, "President Johnson's Special Message to the Congress: The American Promise (video and transcript) March 15, 1965," *LBJ Presidential Library*, http://www.lbjlibrary.org/lyndon-baines-johnson/speeches-films/president-johnsons-special-message-to-the-congress-the-

american-promise [accessed February 11, 2018]

28. Frederick D. Drake, Lynn R. Nelson, ed., *States' Rights and American Federalism: A Documentary History* (Westport, CT: Greenwood Press, 1999) p. 206

29. *Public Papers of the Presidents of the United States: Lyndon B. Johnson January 1 to May 31; 1965,* p. 107

30. Hope Yen, "U.S. poverty on track to rise to highest since 1960s," *Associated Press/Yahoo! News*, July 23, 2012; https://www.yahoo.com/news/us-poverty-track-rise-highest-since-1960s-112946547--finance.html?_esi=1 [accessed February 11, 2018]

31. Michael D. Tanner, "Obama Encouraging Americans to Get on Welfare," *CATO Institute,* July 18, 2012; https://www.cato.org/publications/commentary/obama-encouraging-americans-get-welfare [accessed February 11, 2018]

32. Adam Bitely, "The failed 'War on Poverty'," *Net Right Daily*, July 25, 2012; http://netrightdaily.com/2012/07/the-failed-war-on-poverty/#ixzz21hWfJHZA [accessed February 11, 2018]

33. Walter E. Williams, "The Black Family Is Struggling, and It's Not Because of Slavery," *The Daily Signal*, September 20, 2017; https://www.dailysignal.com/2017/09/20/black-family-struggling-not-slavery [accessed

February 11, 2018]

34. Walter E. Williams, "The Welfare State's Legacy," *Creators Syndicate, Inc.*, September 20, 2017; https://www.creators.com/read/walter-williams/09/17/the-welfare-states-legacy [accessed February 11, 2018]

35. Walter E. Williams, "The Black Family Is Struggling, and It's Not Because of Slavery," *The Daily Signal*, September 20, 2017; https://www.dailysignal.com/2017/09/20/black-family-struggling-not-slavery [accessed February 11, 2018]

36. Robert Rector, "How Welfare Undermines Marriage and What to Do About It," *The Heritage Foundation*, November 17, 2014; https://www.heritage.org/welfare/report/how-welfare-undermines-marriage-and-what-do-about-it [accessed February 11, 2018]

37. Ibid.

38. Ibid.

39. Ibid.

40. Stephen Dinan, "Welfare spending jumps 32% during Obama's presidency," *The Washington Times*, October 18, 2012; https://www.washingtontimes.com/news/2012/oct/18/welfare-spending-jumps-32-percent-four-years/ [accessed February 11, 2018]

41. Andrew M. Allison, W. Cleon Skousen, and M. Richard Maxfield, *The Real Benjamin Franklin*, (Washington D.C.: National Center for Constitutional Studies, 2009) p. 496-497

• 7. Barack Obama

1.   Jerome R. Corsi, Ph.D., *The Obama Nation: Leftist Politics and the Cult of Personality* (New York: Threshold Editions, 2008) p. 145

2.   "Media Inquiries," *The University of Chicago: The Law School*, https://www.law.uchicago.edu/media [accessed February 12, 2018]

3.   Thom Lambert, "Former Obama Law Student Speaks Out," *Fox News Nation*, April 5, 2012; http://nation.foxnews.com/thom-lambert/2012/04/05/former-obama-law-student-speaks-out [accessed February 12, 2018]

4.   Breitbart News Staff, "Former Obama Student: Obama's Ignorance of Constitution Embarrassing," *Breitbart*, April 4, 2012; http://www.breitbart.com/big-government/2012/04/04/former-obama-student-obamas-ignorance-of-constitution-embarrassing/ [accessed February 20, 2018]

5.   Susan Merrill Squier, *Poultry Science, Chicken Culture: A Partial Alphabet* (New Brunswick, NJ: Rutgers University Press, 2011) p. 187

6.   Noni Ellison-Southall, "My View: When the president was my professor," *Schools of Thought*, February 25, 2013; http://schoolsofthought.blogs.cnn.com/2013/02/25/my-view-when-the-president-was-my-

professor/ [accessed February 12, 2018]

7. Pratik Chougule, "Barack Obama: The Great Divider," *The National Interest*, December 31, 2016; http://nationalinterest.org/feature/barack-obama-the-great-divider-17791 [accessed February 12, 2018]

8. Thomas Sowell, "A Post-Racial President?" *Jewish World Review*, July 28, 2009; http://jewishworldreview.com/cols/sowell072809.php3 [accessed February 12, 2018]

9. Saul D. Alinsky, *Rules for Radicals: A Pragmatic Primer for Realistic Radicals* (New York: Vintage Books, 1971) *a*. p. 116; *b*. p. 130; *c*. p. 131

10. Sol Stern, "The Shared Agendas of George Soros and Barack Obama," *Manhattan Institute*, February 2011; http://www.manhattan-institute.org/html/stern__s.htm [accessed February 12, 2018] . . . later accessed when link became inactive at: http://www.discoverthenetworks.org/viewSubCategory.asp?id=1276

11. Charles Johnson, "Full audio of 1998 'redistribution' speech: Obama saw welfare recipients as 'majority coalition'," *Daily Caller*, September 24, 2012; http://dailycaller.com/2012/09/24/full-audio-of-1998-redistribution-speech-obama-saw-welfare-recipients-as-majority-coalition [accessed February 12, 2018]

12. Cynthia Gordy, "Obama Weighs In on Occupy Wall Street," *The Root*, October 6, 2011; http://www.theroot.com/blogs/predatory-lending/obama-weighs-occupy-wall-street [accessed February 12, 2018] . . . later accessed when link became inactive at: https://www.theroot.com/obama-weighs-in-on-occupy-wall-street-1790884006

13. Kerry Picket, "Obama – 'If you've got a business -- you didn't build that. Somebody else made that happen'," *The Washington Times*, July 15, 2012; https://www.washingtontimes.com/blog/watercooler/2012/jul/15/picketvideo-obama-if-youve-got-business-you-didnt-/ [accessed February 12, 2018]

14. Ezra Klein, "Obama: The VOX Conversation – Part one: Domestic Policy," *VOX*, January 23, 2015; https://www.vox.com/a/barack-obama-interview-vox-conversation/obama-domestic-policy-transcript [accessed February 12, 2018]

15. Ibid.

16. Ibid.

17. Ibid.

18. Ibid.

19. Ibid.

20. Video: "Clinton still believes 'it takes a village' to be 'stronger together'," *MSNBC*, July 28, 2016; https://www.msnbc.com/msnbc-quick-

cuts/watch/clinton-still-believes-it-takes-a-village-734428227770 [accessed February 15, 2018]

21. Discover the Networks, "This Is Barack Obama," *Discover the Networks*, page 48; http://www.discoverthenetworks.org/Articles/This%20Is%20Barack%20Obama.pdf [accessed February 12, 2018]

22. Ronald Kessler, "Barack Obama's Racist Church," *NewsMax*, January 7, 2008; https://www.newsmax.com/ronaldkessler/obama-church-racism/2008/01/07/id/322582/ [accessed February 12, 2018]

23. Paulina Dedaj, "Congressional Black Caucus buried 2005 Obama-Farrakhan photo, photographer says," *Fox News*, January 25, 2018; http://www.foxnews.com/politics/2018/01/25/congressional-black-caucus-tried-to-bury-2005-obama-farrakhan-photo-photographer-says.html [accessed February 12, 2018]

24. "National Council of La Raza's Public Funding," *Judicial Watch*, 2011; http://www.judicialwatch.org/files/documents/2011/NCLRfunding.pdf [accessed February 12, 2018]

25. Justin Eliott, "Obama cracks down on abuses by big-city police departments," *Salon*, May 30, 2001; https://www.salon.com/2011/05/30/justice_department_civil_rights_police/ [accessed February 12, 2018]

26. U.S. Justice Department, "Department of Justice Report Regarding the Criminal Investigation into the Shooting Death of Michael Brown by Ferguson, Missouri Police Officer Darren Wilson," *U.S. Department of Justice*, March 4, 2015; http://www.justice.gov/sites/default/files/opa/press-releases/attachments/2015/03/04/doj_report_on_shooting_of_michael_brown_1.pdf [accessed February 15, 2018]

27. Mark Berman, "The seven racist e-mails the Justice Department highlighted in its report on Ferguson police," *The Washington Post*, March 4, 2015; https://www.washingtonpost.com/news/post-nation/wp/2015/03/04/the-seven-racist-e-mails-the-justice-department-highlighted-in-its-report-on-ferguson-police/?utm_term=.64a20a7cd969 [accessed February 15, 2018]

28. Ashley Rae Goldenberg, "Defense Department: The Bible, Constitution And Declaration of Independence Perpetuate Sexism," *The Daily Caller*, April 13, 2015; http://dailycaller.com/2015/04/13/defense-department-the-bible-constitution-and-declaration-of-independence-all-perpetuate-sexism/2/ [accessed February 15, 2018]

29. Heather Higgins, "Barack Obama's Poor Understanding of the Constitution," *U.S. News & World Report*, November 3, 2008;

https://www.usnews.com/opinion/articles/20
08/11/03/barack-obamas-poor-
understanding-of-the-constitution [accessed
February 15, 2018]

30. John Woolley and Gerhard Peters,
"Executive Orders: J.Q. Adams – Trump,"
*The American Presidency Project –
University of California at Santa Barbara*,
April 26, 2017
http://www.presidency.ucsb.edu/executive_or
ders.php?year=2017 [accessed February 15,
2018]

31. Barack Obama, "Remarks by the President
on the Economy -- Austin, TX; Paramount
Theatre," *Obama White House*, July 10,
2014;
https://obamawhitehouse.archives.gov/the-
press-office/2014/07/10/remarks-president-
economy-austin-tx [accessed February 15,
2018]

32. "Obama on Executive Actions: 'I've Got A
Pen And I've Got A Phone'," *CBS DC*,
January 14, 2014;
http://washington.cbslocal.com/2014/01/14/o
bama-on-executive-actions-ive-got-a-pen-
and-ive-got-a-phone/ [accessed February 15,
2018]

33. Gregory Korte, "Obama issues 'executive
orders by another name'," *USA Today*,
December 16, 2014;
https://www.usatoday.com/story/news/politic
s/2014/12/16/obama-presidential-

memoranda-executive-orders/20191805/
[accessed February 9, 2018]

34. Ibid.
35. Ibid.
36. Ibid.
37. Elizabeth Slattery and Andrew Kloster, "An Executive Unbound: The Obama Administration's Unilateral Actions," *The Heritage Foundation*, February 12, 2014; https://www.heritage.org/the-constitution/report/executive-unbound-the-obama-administrations-unilateral-actions [accessed February 9, 2018]
38. Ibid.
39. Ibid.
40. Ibid.
41. Ibid.
42. Ibid.
43. Ibid.
44. AWR Hawkins, "Stimulus Money: A Slush Fund for Unions and Democrats," *Breitbart*, May 4, 2012; www.breitbart.com/big-government/2012/05/04/stimulus-money-a-slush-fund-for-unions-and-democrats/ [accessed February 14, 2018]
45. "Quality of Life Rankings: Measuring states' natural and social environments," *U.S. News & World Report*, https://www.usnews.com/news/best-states/rankings/quality-of-life [accessed February 27, 2018]
46. Associated Press, "$1.7-billion payment to

Iran was all cash due to effectiveness of sanctions, White House Says," *Los Angeles Times*, September 7, 2016; http://www.latimes.com/nation/nationnow/la-na-iran-payment-cash-20160907-snap-story.html [accessed February 15, 2018]

47. Mark Hemingway, "$162 million in stimulus funds unaccounted for," *Washington Examiner*, October 4, 2010; www.washingtonexaminer.com/162-million-in-stimulus-funds-unaccounted-for/article/132356 [accessed February 15, 2018]

48. AWR Hawkins, "Stimulus Money: A Slush Fund for Unions and Democrats," *Breitbart*, May 4, 2012; www.breitbart.com/big-government/2012/05/04/stimulus-money-a-slush-fund-for-unions-and-democrats/ [accessed February 15, 2018]

49. Douglas V. Gibbs, "Myth #19: Being Born in the United States Satisfies the Definition of Natural Born Citizen," *Political Pistachio*, September 19, 2011; *http://politicalpistachio.blogspot.com/2011/0 9/myth-19-being-born-in-united-states.html*

• **Post Script: Abraham Lincoln**

1. "Life and Legacy," *The John Marshall Foundation*, http://www.johnmarshallfoundation.org/john-marshall/life-legacy/ [accessed January 10,

2018]
2. "Abraham Lincoln," *Biography.com*, https://www.biography.com/people/abraham-lincoln-9382540 [accessed January 10, 2018]
3. Doris Kearns Goodwin, *Team of Rivals: The Political Genius of Abraham Lincoln* (New York, Simon & Schuster, 2006) p. 57
4. Ibid. p. 88
5. Ibid. p. 89
6. Ibid. p. 91
7. Ibid. p. 103
8. Ibid. p. 105
9. Thomas J. DiLorenzo, *The Real Lincoln: A New Look at Abraham Lincoln, His Agenda, and an Unnecessary War* (New York: Three Rivers Press, 2003) p. 3
10. Abraham Lincoln, "Selected Quotations by Abraham Lincoln," *Abraham Lincoln Online: Speeches and Writings*, http://www.abrahamlincolnonline.org/lincoln/speeches/quotes.htm [accessed January 10, 2018]
11. Thomas J. DiLorenzo, *The Real Lincoln: A New Look at Abraham Lincoln, His Agenda, and an Unnecessary War* (New York: Three Rivers Press, 2003) p. 54
12. James Madison, "Madison's Veto of federal public works bill, 1817," http://www.constitution.org/jm/18170303_veto.htm . . . link no longer accessible, data transferred to http://politicalpistachio.blogspot.com/2018/0

2/madisons-veto-of-federal-public-works.html (and available on pages 253-256 of this book)

13.   Milton and Rose Friedman, *Free to Choose: A Personal Statement* (New York: Harcourt Brace & Company, 1980) p. 131

14.   Frank J. Williams, *Judging Lincoln* (Carbondale, IL: Southern Illinois University Press, 2002) p. 77

15.   Thomas J. DiLorenzo, *The Real Lincoln: A New Look at Abraham Lincoln, His Agenda, and an Unnecessary War* (New York: Three Rivers Press, 2003) p. 132

16.   Ibid. p. 132-133

17.   Ibid.

• Index

McCarthy, Joseph; 139

McCullough v. Maryland; 62, 77-79, 108

Mercantilism; 51, 53, 96, 205

Mexican-American War; 21

Milk, Harvey; 27

Monroe, James; 53, 61

Moore, Michael; 30-31

Mortgage Bubble; (see "Housing Bubble")

Mugabe, Robert; 24

Muslim; (see "Islam")

N

NAACP; 15

Nader, Ralph; 27

National Security; 22, 24, 25

National Treasure (movie); 194

Nationalism; 18, 63, 102, 200, 205, 206

Natural Born Citizen; 183, 224

Natural Rights; 190

Nazi Germany; 22

# #

Made in the USA
Columbia, SC
03 May 2021